Creating a Culture for High-Performing Schools

Creating a Culture for High-Performing Schools

A Comprehensive Approach to School Reform, Dropout Prevention, and Bullying Behavior

Second Edition

Cletus R. Bulach,
Fred C. Lunenburg,
and Les Potter

ROWMAN & LITTLEFIELD EDUCATION
Lanham • New York • Toronto • Plymouth, UK

Published by Rowman & Littlefield Education
A division of Rowman & Littlefield Publishers, Inc.
A wholly owned subsidary of The Rowman & Littlefield Publishing Group, Inc.
4501 Forbes Boulevard, Suite 200, Lanham, Maryland 20706
http://www.rowmaneducation.com

Estover Road, Plymouth PL6 7PY, United Kingdom

British Library Cataloguing in Publication Information Available

Library of Congress Cataloging-in-Publication Data

Bulach, Cletus R.
  Creating a culture for high-performing schools : a comprehensive approach to school reform, dropout prevention, and bullying behavior / Cletus R. Bulach, Fred C. Lunenburg, and Les Potter. — 2nd ed.
    p. cm.
  ISBN 978-1-61048-321-6 (cloth : alk. paper) — ISBN 978-1-61048-322-3 (pbk. : alk. paper) — ISBN 978-1-61048-323-0 (electronic)
  1. School improvement programs—United States.   2. Academic achievement—United States.   3. School environment—United States.   I. Lunenburg, Frederick C.
II. Potter, Les, 1948– III. Title.
LB2822.82.B85   2011
371.2'07—dc23   2011028071

Table of Contents

Preface

PURPOSE OF THE BOOK

The most recent report by the National Center on Education and the Economy (2007) called for comprehensive school reform. The report stated that there is a growing mismatch between the type of students our schools are producing and the needs of the economy.

In *Creating a Culture for High-Performing Schools*, the authors describe a comprehensive school reform approach that reduces resistance to school reform and increases the likelihood of creating a caring learning community. Creating a "high-performing" school is an organizational approach to school reform that creates a distinctly different school culture and climate than can be found in existing schools. The authors detail a mission and vision for a comprehensive school reform that involves all stakeholders and leads to high performance.

The authors believed that the 1st edition of this book was too eclectic. There were thirteen chapters for principals, four for teachers, and two for counselors. In this 2nd edition, the book has been revised specifically for school administrators, although teachers can also use the information to create high performing classrooms. The 2nd edition also addresses bullying behavior and how to reduce it. Since publication of the 1st edition, four schools have implemented one part of the school reform, and pre- and post-implementation data are provided.

ORIGIN OF THE VISION AND MISSION

Many schools have a mission of developing a positive school culture designed to improve the quality of instruction, leading to high student test scores; however, it is often the case that the vision to achieve that mission has not been successfully communicated to all stakeholders. During the past 40 years, one of the authors, Dr. Clete Bulach, has held positions as a teacher, principal, superintendent, and college professor in a department of educational leadership. He also had difficulty communicating a vision of how to create a culture that leads to high performance on the part of faculty and students.

Based on his experience as the external evaluation consultant for character education for Georgia and West Virginia, that has changed. In the fall of 2001, the West Virginia Legislature passed HB 2208 mandating the evaluation of the character education program of every school district in the state. Bulach was awarded the contract to evaluate each school district in the state during the 2002–2003 school year.

Character and culture survey data were collected in 65 high schools, 65 middle schools, and 65 elementary schools. He visited one school in each district and interviewed students, teachers, and administrators. During the interview, each of these stakeholder groups was asked what they liked and did not like about their school and what they liked and did not like about their school's character education program.

In Georgia, four years (1999–2002) of culture/climate and character data from faculty and students at six high schools, seven middle schools, and twelve elementary schools were also collected. In reflecting on the data collected in these two states, a clear vision emerged of how to create a culture for a high-performing school. This vision includes the concepts of servant leadership, organizational culture and climate, the use of authority and power, community building, character education, and the use of a variety of strategies and diagnostic tools.

WHAT IS A HIGH-PERFORMING SCHOOL?

A high-performing school is described as one where student achievement is high and student and teacher absenteeism is low. Student behavior is such that teachers seldom have to control them or tell them what to do. This results in greater time on task, improved achievement scores, improved teacher morale, lower teacher absenteeism, a lower student dropout rate, reduced bullying behavior, and improved parental support.

Another distinct feature of a high-performing school is that the student peer group is a positive rather than a negative force. The end result is a school culture where faculty and students trust and care about each other, and there is a cooperative attitude. The focus is on what can be done to help one another, and everyone is involved in the decision-making process. The end result is students who graduate as responsible and productive citizens.

The key concept that changes the existing school culture is to give control to students without giving up control. The greatest fear of a teacher or school administrator is to lose control of discipline. We will provide data at the classroom and school level that proves educators can give control to students without giving up control. Teachers who had to stop teaching a number of times found that they could teach almost without interruption.

Three elementary schools and one middle school have implemented one part of this reform. After one semester of implementation, student off-task behavior had decreased by 76 percent. This allowed teachers more time to teach and less interruption of the learning process. There was also a reduction in office referrals, allowing school administrators more time to be out and about.

The culture of control in each classroom and the entire school can be changed. Students will control each other, not only in the classroom, but in the bathrooms, hallways, lunchroom, and so on. This is **one** of the **four major changes** that create a high performing school culture. Another word could be used. It could be called a "Citizenship" school, because in this school culture students help each other, dropouts are reduced, and bullying behavior is reduced.

WHO SHOULD READ THIS BOOK?

This book contains valuable information for school administrators, and members of boards of education. They must be involved for a comprehensive school reform to work. Teachers, however, can also implement many of the ideas, strategies, and processes in their classrooms, even though other teachers and the administration are not involved. Professors in colleges of education will also find this book a useful supplementary text. Anyone who is critical of the current education process will find this an interesting read with its novel approach to the creation of a school's culture and climate.

ORGANIZATION OF THE BOOK

This book is divided into three parts: In part I, chapters 1 through 5, the authors describe a school reform process to create this culture. In part I, there are four distinct phases for creating a culture and climate for a high-performing school.

The four types of school cultures observed during on-site visits to school districts in West Virginia are described in chapter 1. There is the "laissez-faire" low-performing school, the "traditional" under-performing school, the "enlightened traditional" above average–performing school, and the high-performing school. A high-performing school is one where faculty and students have cultivated a feeling of community, and they work together in a cooperative environment to help each other grow and become more responsible citizens. Implementing the high performing school culture is **Phase 1** of this comprehensive school reform.

Phase 2 requires the involvement of all faculty in a four-step process for shaping the culture of the school. The desired culture is one where there is a caring learning environment and where students and faculty are open and trusting with each other. This is the focus of chapters 2 and 3.

Phase 3 is a continuation of the process for creating a high-performing school. This phase requires the appropriate use of power to motivate and control students and all constituents in the school environment. There are five freeing forms of power that tend to improve the culture and climate and four controlling forms of power that, if overused, cause a poor culture and climate; however, if they are not used when needed, a poor culture and climate will also result. The appropriate use and misuse of the freeing and controlling forms of power and their role in creating a high-performing school are the focus of chapter 4.

Phase 4 describes a character education program that involves the students, faculty, staff, parents, and community. This character education program drives the preceding three phases and complements the feeling of community created in the high-performing school. How to implement this character education program, which does not require a curriculum or additional time during the school day, is the subject of chapter 5. In part I, the authors provide a detailed description of how to create a climate and culture for a high-performing school.

In part II and chapter 6, the authors describe how the culture created in part I can be enhanced. In this chapter, practical strategies are detailed that can be taken to reduce bullying behavior and further improve a school's culture and climate.

In part III, the authors provide a variety of other strategies and processes designed to assist in improving the culture and climate of a high-performing school. In chapters 7 through 10, the authors describe the leadership skills needed to create a high-performing school. Chapter 7 is designed specifically for school principals and describes a reconceptualization of the role of the principal required for a high-performing school. Strategies and processes that encourage the learning of all students and the professional growth of faculty are described in chapters 8 and 9.

In these chapters, the authors describe a set of intergroup processes often overlooked in other books on school leadership. The interpersonal relationship that develops between faculty is a crucial element of the reform implementation process. Many of the strategies and activities are also applicable for use at the classroom level, because interpersonal relationships are also a crucial element between teachers and students in the learning process.

In chapter 10, the authors provide a detailed description on how to conduct a parent-student-teacher (three-way) conference. This chapter is included because the authors believe it is one way to show students we trust them to be responsible and take charge of the learning process. In the early chapters of this book we shared our thoughts on the importance of giving control to students without giving up control. The three-way conference is another example of how to do that.

REFERENCE

National Center on Education and the Economy. (2007). Tough choices or tough times: The report of the new commission on the skills of the American workforce. San Francisco: John Wiley & Sons.

Part I

School Reform Processes

Four distinct phases for creating a high-performing school are described in chapters 1 through 5. Each phase can stand alone, but the phases build on one another. This is a comprehensive school reform that is designed to improve a school's culture and climate. It is also designed to improve student test scores, prevent student dropouts, and reduce bullying behavior.

Chapter 1

Four Types of School Culture

Phase One (Change the existing culture of control)

In this chapter, four distinct types of school cultures and the leadership style that creates that type are described. How to implement Phase 1 of the high performing school culture will also be described. The four types are:

1. the laissez-faire school culture is an underperforming school (2 percent–5 percent)
2. the traditional school culture is a low-performing school (60 percent–75 percent)
3. the enlightened traditional school culture is an above average performing school (10 percent–15 percent)
4. the high-performing school culture (2 percent–5 percent)

These four types of school cultures were observed while making on-site visits and conducting interviews with faculty and students at 65 individual schools in West Virginia.* All schools, because of the values and beliefs of the school community, have an established culture. As a result of this under-lying culture, various rules and expectations are in place. A key component of any school's climate is the control culture. How faculty and students are controlled determines the type of school culture and climate. In addition to the control culture, the leadership style of the principal often plays a key

---

*Cletus R. Bulach was serving as the external evaluator for the West Virginia character education grant while conducting these interviews and on-site visits in (2002–2005). He logged 5000 miles and spent 5 months in every school district in the State. One school in each district was visited. Two sets of students were interviewed. One was the student leadership team and the other set was a randomly selected set of classroom students. The teachers at each school were interviewed using a "force field analysis" technique (described in chapter 2).

3

role in shaping a school's culture. Keep in mind that a school can be a blend between two or more cultures.

In this chapter, the authors also describe the role of control for implementing Phase 1 of the reform process for creating a high-performing school. Prior to implementing the "high-performing" school culture (Phase 1), school officials must first identify the type of school culture that exists at their school. Describing the four types of school cultures assists with that process.

THE LAISSEZ-FAIRE, LOW-PERFORMING SCHOOL

A laissez-faire school is a low-performing school and it is characterized by a lack of control. There are not many schools with this type of culture, but they do exist. Based on our collective experience, we estimate that the number of schools with this type of culture is around 2–5 percent. The morning that I (Bulach) entered the office of a school of this type, the front office was noisy, and there were a number of people waiting for the secretary to admit them to school. The principal, who could have been assisting with the overflow, was in her office. I patiently waited until the secretary had time for me. When told that I was the evaluator of their character education program, she rang the principal, and I was ushered into her office. Before I could enter, someone came in from the hall and said there was a bunch of students in the hallway. The principal went to the hall and said to the students, "What is going on?" A student said that "Coach is not here to let us in our room!"

The principal at this school did not have a procedure in place to make sure that all teachers had arrived and were at their posts to supervise students. Later that day, I asked to meet with the teacher who was responsible for student council, as I wanted to interview the student leadership team about their perceptions of the school and their character education program. The teacher was not in his room. Instead he was supervising the class of another teacher, who was out sick. I found that teacher in the teachers' lounge. The principal of the school was totally unaware of this incident.

In walking through the school to check for evidence of a character education program, I noticed a number of students in the hallway. I personally escorted one student to his room only to find him sitting in a locker on another floor 10 minutes later. As I walked into classrooms and observed what teachers were doing, some were teaching, and others were sitting at their desks while the students talked and were off-task. In a laissez-faire school, the principal does not have procedures in place to control the faculty, and the teachers do not have procedures in place to control the students.

A variation of this type is a school where procedures are in place, but teachers do not follow them, and the principal does not follow through to make sure the procedure is carried out. The leadership style tends to be nondirective, and the principal tends to ask people to do things, However, there tends to be little follow-through to make sure the request is acted on. Faculty and students tend to be self-serving, and there is an absence of servant leadership. Servant leadership will be described in detail in chapter 2.

In interviewing students and teachers at this school, some of the negative comments were as follows:

- Some teachers punish the whole class when one student is the problem.
- Teachers and the principal have favorites. They will punish some kids and the same thing goes unpunished for the ones they like—particularly the dress code.
- The dress code and other rules are not enforced. Some teachers look the other way.
- The punishment does not always fit the crime.
- New students are not accepted.
- There is a lack of organization.
- People here are judgmental.

THE TRADITIONAL, UNDERPERFORMING SCHOOL

A second type of school culture is a traditional school, and it is characterized by a heavy emphasis on control. It is an underperforming school, and in our opinion 60–75 percent of schools have this type of culture. The principal and the administrative team are very much in control. Teachers are subordinate to the leadership team and are not involved in the decision-making process. There is a faculty handbook, and there are procedures established for everything that is supposed to happen at that school. Lesson plans are submitted on a daily basis, and everything is checked to make sure everyone is following procedures. The same is true for students. Teachers are very much in control of what happens in each classroom.

Students are not involved in what happens at the school. There is no student council or student leadership team. If one does exist, it has no decision-making power. It is a rubber stamp for the administration. The leadership style is directive and position, reward, and coercion are three forms of power used to control students and faculty. Coercion power in the form of punishment, however, is the most frequently used form of power. There are six other forms of power in addition to these three. The nine forms of power, and their use and misuse are described in chapter 4 (Phase 3).

In one such school, when I asked the students what they liked about their school, they had little to say. Several comments about what they liked were, "When school is out!" and "When I get off the bus!" When asked what they did not like, they were hesitant to talk. One student asked, "Will we get in trouble if we tell you things?" When I assured them that all comments were anonymous, and no one would know who said what, it was difficult to keep them quiet. Everyone wanted to talk. Their frustrated and angry comments were as follows:

- Some teachers are nice but a lot of them are not nice.
- Some teachers cuss and call students names.
- Teachers have favorites. They will punish some kids, and the same thing goes unpunished for the ones they like.
- The teachers have double standards. They won't let us do things, but they do them. (Eating and drinking in their room was an example given.)
- The principal is mean.
- I do not like anything about it.
- The teachers put us down and ignore us.
- The teachers do not help us when we need it.

In this type of school, faculty and the administration use grades and punishment to motivate the students. If students do not study, they receive an F. If they do not obey rules, they are punished. These are forms of extrinsic motivation and one of the major reasons why the schools are underperforming. Students tend to do what they have to do to stay out of trouble and get the grade they want. In talking with a teacher in one of these schools, she commented that, "If you give the students any freedom, they get out of control." The administration and teachers in this type of school have to constantly be on watch to make sure students do what they are supposed to do.

The majority of schools in the United States fall into this category. Silva and Mackin (2002) wrote:

Next to prisons, high schools are the least democratic institutions in our American society. They are cursed by a tradition of hypocrisy—teaching and espousing democratic doctrine within the classroom, but doing it in a highly controlled authoritarian manner that makes the actual practice of democratic principles largely nonexistent anywhere in the school. (p. 1)

Their opinion is supported by Kohn (2006, 2004), who stated that there is an over-reliance on punishment as a way of disciplining students who do not follow rules. He wrote that school officials' response to discipline with ever-harsher measures is counterproductive. The next type of school culture attempts to address this over-reliance on punishment.

THE ENLIGHTENED TRADITIONAL, ABOVE AVERAGE–PERFORMING SCHOOL

A third type of school culture is an enlightened traditional school, and it is an above average–performing school. We estimate that approximately 10 percent–15 percent of schools have some variation of this type of culture. The principal and administrative teams are also very much in control; however, they have created incentives or reinforcers for faculty and students to control themselves. Instead of relying on position and coercion to control faculty and students, they have an established system of rewards to encourage faculty and students to control themselves. This is an attempt to shift control from the leaders to subordinates. Some examples of incentives or rewards are:

- Teacher of the year: Teachers are recognized at a board meeting and given a parking spot close to the school entrance as a way to encourage teachers to go the extra mile.
- Leadership team: teachers are chosen by the principal to provide advice and assist with the communication process when needed.
- Student of the month: Each teacher has a student of the month, or sometimes only one is chosen for the entire school as a way to recognize attendance, character behavior, citizenship, and so forth. Other variations can be students who are recognized at the end of a grading period, the end of the semester, or the end of the year.
- Points system: Students who do what they are supposed to do regarding homework, attendance, and behavior earn points. These points can be cashed in at the student store for pencils, paper, or other school-related items or for treats in the cafeteria.
- Redirects, reminders, or violations: Students who do not do what they are supposed to do are given a redirect. The redirect can be for any rule infraction or failure to exhibit a behavior related to a character trait. If a student receives three redirects in one day, a punishment is incurred. At the end of a grading period, all students who have incurred no punishments in the form of office referrals or less than three redirects are rewarded with a field trip or something else that the students have requested. One school has a "movie madness" afternoon where students select a movie they want to watch, and business partners provide food and drinks.

- Caught doing good: A certificate is given to students who do good deeds. This can be related to the character word for the month or any other deed that a teacher deems worthy of recognition. Some schools provide treats or rewards for each certificate and recognize students during morning announcements.

In the enlightened traditional school, both punishment and reward are used to motivate and/or control students. The motivation is still extrinsic, but there is an improvement in student behavior. According to the research of Marzano, Marzano, and Pickering (2003), there is a 24 percent increase in student misbehavior where there are no consequences, a 28 percent decrease where there are consequences, a 31 percent decrease if there are rewards for positive behavior, and a 33 percent decrease if punishment and rewards are both used.

Marzano and colleagues (2003) stated that, "The guiding principle for disciplinary interventions is that they should include a healthy balance between negative consequences for inappropriate behavior and positive consequences for appropriate behavior" (p. 40). Kohn (2006), however, stated that this type of discipline does not help students to grow to be responsible students. He believes that students should control their behavior because it is the right thing to do and not because of a reward.

The controversy over the use of rewards has been ongoing. According to Sergiovanni and Starratt (2002), the use of rewards is not a good practice because student behavior is motivated for external reasons, that is, the desired behavior occurs because of the reward and not because it is the right thing to do. They believe that students should not be rewarded (external motivation) for a behavior that they are supposed to do because it is the right thing to do (internal motivation). Giving a reward (external) for something they are supposed to do (internal) extinguishes the internal motivation. Intermittent reward, however, according to these theorists does not extinguish internal motivation.

Several schools were observed using intermittent rewards for students "caught doing good." They received a "caught doing good" certificate and personal recognition. The certificate was put in a box, and at the end of the week, several names were drawn from the box. Those students received a prize from the school's business partners. One school drew two names and their business partner, a bank, gave each student a $50 savings bond.

Another variation of "caught doing good" is the ability of students to trade in a number of "caught doing good" certificates to remove a redirect or reminder. In some schools, students who have more than three redirects, reminders, or violations are excluded from the end-of-grading-period reward. The intent here is to present students with the opportunity to get back into the good graces of school officials. Supposedly, once a student knows they are excluded from the end-of-grading-period reward, there is no incentive for them to behave other than traditional discipline procedures.

The ability to trade "caught doing good" certificates for rule infractions is an incentive for the so-called "bad actors" to continue trying to improve their behavior. In schools that use point systems instead of certificates, students can use points to buy back a violation or redirect. This practice encourages desirable behavior by rewarding it while continuing to punish undesirable behavior.

Many enlightened traditional schools do not have a plan in place to motivate students who have lost the chance to take part in the end-of-report-period reward. This is a mistake as there is no motivation for these students to behave once they have lost the opportunity to take part in the reward. A system should be put in place so they can earn back the right to take part. One of the comments frequently heard during the student interviews when asked about their character education program was that it had no effect on the bad actors. These bad actors are typically 5 percent to 7 percent of the students, and they are the students who make it difficult for teachers to teach and other students to learn. A plan has to be developed to encourage these students to control their disruptive behavior.

An interesting variation of "caught doing good" was observed at a middle school, and it involved the use of a character bulletin board. Teachers who saw a student doing something representative of the character trait being taught would put a post-it note with the student's name on the bulletin board. In the morning, before classes started, students looked at the bulletin board to see if their name was there. If it was, they took it to the teacher who put it there, and then three things happened.

1. The teacher verbally reinforced the student's positive behavior.
2. The student was given a treat.
3. The post-it note was put in a jar in the office.

A post-it was periodically drawn from the jar, and that student and the teacher were given a prize. The teacher's reward was a free period while the principal taught the class. The students' treat or prize can be as small as a pencil or an ice cream at lunch or a McDonald's meal or something larger from another business partner.

The intriguing part was the interest and excitement created by not rewarding the behavior when it happened. Instead the students had to check the bulletin board each morning to see who was caught being good. When students at this school were interviewed, they said they really liked the character bulletin board and the excitement it generated when they took their name off the board and went to the teacher, cook, or other person who put their name there to find out what they had done. And teachers liked having the principal take their class for a period.

Marzano and colleagues (2003) stated that behavior limits need to be established, and a record-keeping system must be in place. In some schools it means having a pencil, finishing homework, having textbooks, raising hands, not getting out of seats unless permitted, walking on the right side of the hall, following the dress code, and so forth. Students with too many violations lose their freedom at lunch. Too many violations can be as few as one to as many as five. Instead of going to lunch and perhaps recess with the other students, misbehaving students get their lunch and report to a separate room where they are counseled on what they have to do to earn back the right to eat lunch with the other students.

In an enlightened traditional school, a system is in place to encourage students and others to control their own behavior. The burden of controlling what people are supposed to do is shared with everyone in the school. Students and faculty are given the freedom to control their own behavior, and incentives are in place to encourage desirable behavior. If students and faculty do not control their own behavior and undesirable behavior is the result, then someone controls them and does something to extinguish the undesirable behavior.

This is in contrast to the traditional school where students and faculty have little freedom—students are controlled by teachers, and teachers are controlled by the administration. They must do what they are supposed to or they will receive admonishment or punishment. The leadership style in an enlightened traditional school tends to be collaborative. The forms of power used are information, personality, ego, and moral power. Position and coercion power are used when the preceding forms of power do not work. Servant leadership can take place in this type of school, but the focus on getting a reward tends to be self-serving. The forms of power and servant leadership will be discussed in detail in chapter 4.

THE HIGH-PERFORMING SCHOOL

A fourth type of school culture is the high-performing school. We estimate that there have to be some schools (2 percent–5 percent) with this type of culture. We do know of the one observed in West Virginia and of several in Indiana that have implemented this reform. The school in West Virginia was the impetus for this chapter and the book. The high-performing school has many of the same features as the enlightened traditional school, but it has added an additional reward for desirable behavior.

While the enlightened traditional school relies on individuals to control their own behavior, the high-performing school creates an incentive or reward for the peer group to help control other students. For example, if there are no redirects, reminders, or violations or less than a prescribed number, the peer group gets a reward. This can take many forms. The peer group can be a class of students, a team, an advisory group, a homeroom, a grade level, or the entire school. The larger the peer group, the more students are involved in controlling the other students.

Ideally, the entire school should be involved, but it has been successful in a single classroom as well. This system requires setting a benchmark for the students to try to reach or stay under. For example, if office referrals for the entire school for a week totaled 100, the benchmark can be set at 50. If the number of office referrals for the next week were under that benchmark, all the students are given a reward. The reward can be a recess, board games, or some other compensation that is a motivator.

In a high-performing school all students receive the reward, whereas in an enlightened traditional school only those students who have behaved responsibly are compensated. In a high-performing school peer pressure on those students who are disruptive does occur. There is also an additional incentive for disruptive students to do what they are supposed to do because they will also enjoy the reward, whereas in the enlightened traditional setting, they are excluded.

Office referrals can be used to establish benchmarks, but a better system uses redirects, reminders, or pink slips. There is a lot of student behavior that does not warrant punishment, but it does interfere with creating a caring learning environment. Responsible student behavior must be encouraged. The redirects, reminders, or pink slips are one way to encourage responsible student behavior without punishing students every time they forget to do what they are supposed to do.

Only one high-performing school was observed during the on-site visits and interviews in West Virginia. School officials at this middle school set a benchmark and reward for each day, as well as an end-of-report-period reward for students with fewer than three redirects during the period. Their benchmark was 25 or fewer redirects for a day. If that benchmark were met, the reward was 10 extra minutes of locker time the next day. This particular school had approximately 350 students, and they met their benchmark on an average of four times per week. On the day of the visit, they had fewer than 10 redirects, and the reward was an extra 10 minutes of free time before dismissal.

When asked to describe a redirect, the principal stated that any time a teacher had to reprimand a student for not raising their hand, running, wearing a cap, talking, and so forth, it was considered a redirect. When asked how state guidelines for time requirements were addressed, the principal stated that students have more "time on task" at his school because teachers had fewer interruptions of the instructional process. He stated that when they started this system 10 years ago, the benchmark was 100 redirects and each year they have lowered the benchmark to the current 25.

While there was only one high-performing school observed, a number of teachers were seen in other schools who used some variation of the high-performing school at the classroom level. Some teachers used movies and popcorn, but this was not a strong motivator because students had often already seen the movie. Some used field trips, which tend to be strong motivators.

The strongest motivator is free time. Students want time to interact with their friends. If the reward is a weekly event, a strong motivator is extra time on Friday to go to the gym or playground and hang out or play games. If the reward for reducing the number redirects is a daily event, five minutes of extra time at recess is a very strong motivator. At the elementary level, the ability to delay gratification is difficult for students. Extra recess is a very strong motivator because they know at the end of the day whether they have met their target. Choosing a reward that will motivate the peer group to become active in controlling each other is extremely important.

An elementary school that was visited had a banner displayed outside the classroom with the fewest redirects for the month. A classroom was visited where a teacher had two jars of marbles. She told her students if they had a good day, she would take a handful of marbles from jar one and put it into jar two. When the jar one was empty and jar two full, the entire class could go to McDonald's for ice cream. She had some other rules regarding the marbles:

1. If they had a bad day, she would remove a handful of marbles from jar two and place them back in jar one or vice versa if they had a good day.
2. If a student did something good, she might take a marble from jar one and place it in jar two.
3. If a student did something bad, she might take a marble out of jar two and place it back in jar one.

Through use of the marbles and the jars, this teacher created a high-performing classroom and an incentive for the students to help each other to behave responsibly. Another variation of this classroom control/incentive technique involved the use of a paper chain. The teacher added a link to the chain when the class did what they were supposed to do. When it reached a certain length, the entire class got a reward. When there were only a few marbles left in jar one or only a few more links to add to the chain, student behavior was wonderful. They worked together because they knew the reward was soon to come.

One interesting observation about the high-performing school or classroom is that it teaches a very important character trait—citizenship. It creates a community within a classroom, grade level, team, or school where students are encouraged to be responsible citizens. They follow rules, obey authority, help each other, intervene when something wrong is about to happen or is happening, and so forth. They learn to recognize undesirable behavior and model desirable behavior.

This type of school creates an environment where students can become responsible citizens. The leadership style, as in an enlightened traditional school, tends to be collaborative. The interesting transformation, however, is that control has been shifted to students. They are being asked to help control each other whereas in the past, it was the teachers and other faculty members' responsibility to control students.

This shift in control changes the peer group from a negative force to a positive force. Berger (2003) wrote: "I was raised with the message that peer pressure was something terrible, something to avoid, something negative. Peer pressure meant kids trying to talk you into smoking cigarettes or taking drugs. I realized after 10 years of teaching that positive peer pressure was the primary reason my classroom was a safe, supportive environment for student learning. Peer pressure wasn't something to be afraid of, to be avoided, but rather to be cultivated in a positive direction." (p. 36) In most classrooms, peer pressure is still a negative force. Changing the existing control culture is a common sense approach to give control to the peer group and make it a positive force.

THE ROLE OF CONTROL IN A HIGH PERFORMING SCHOOL

A culture has been created in most schools where control issues are a major factor. Boards control superintendents, who control central office, who control principals, who control teachers, who control students. It is all about control. They believe they have to have control and in fact **they do have to control.** Losing control is one of the greatest fears of any educator, whether teacher, administrator, or board member. Control has to be there! **Learning cannot occur in a school where there is not a highly controlled environment.**

That being said, think for a minute about how you feel when you have lost control or are not in control versus how you feel when you are in control. It is as different as night and day. In a school environment, everyone is in a highly controlled environment. While everyone wants to be in an environment where things are under control, very few people like to be controlled.

A successful marriage or relationship has both elements: It should be a controlled setting that gives control. If a marriage or relationship is to be successful, someone has to be in control of what happens. However, if the other person or people in the relationship feel like they are being controlled, they will not be happy. It is a universal principle that human beings like to have some feeling of control.

That is not the case with schools across the country. Students must follow the rules and study what is on their schedule. Students are controlled and have little control over what happens. That is one of the major reasons why many are unmotivated and dropout. The lack of motivation is also one of the major causes of low test scores.

Teachers are also in a highly controlled environment and must do what the administration tells them to do. Administrators must carry out the mandates of their states' DOE. No one, whether teacher, student, or principal, likes to be in a situation where they feel controlled. Yet that is what is happening in school after school across the United States. This causes a number of problems resulting in low test scores, student absenteeism, poor school culture and climate, and high teacher absenteeism on Mondays and Fridays.

How does this relate to the culture of control that exists in schools? When student misbehavior occurs, students do nothing because they expect the administration or teachers to control the situation. It is not okay for students to intervene because they are in a highly controlled environment. Students are controlled and are not expected to exert control on other students. If a student were to exert control on another student, they would be asked: "Who do you think you are?" They might be called the teacher's pet or something else. A culture has been created where students are not encouraged to control other students. There may be schools that are exceptions to this generalization? One exception would be JROTC units where students are expected to control underclassmen. Perhaps that is why they are so successful? Montessori schools could be another exception.

One interesting observation about the high-performing school or classroom is that students are given control, but control has not been given up. It also teaches a very important character trait—citizenship. It creates a community within a classroom, grade level, team, or school where students are encouraged to control each other and be responsible citizens. They follow rules, obey authority, help each other, intervene when something wrong is about to happen or is happening, and so forth. They learn to recognize undesirable behavior and model desirable behavior. They realize that control has been shifted to students, and it is their responsibility to intervene when their peers' behavior is inappropriate. In the three other types of school cultures, controlling students' behavior is the responsibility of the faculty and the administration.

The existing culture of control in most schools creates another problem. That problem is bullying behavior. When bullying behavior occurs, the other students become bystanders as they watch it take place. According to Beane and Bulach (2009) and Beane (2009), 53 percent of students reported that they stand and watch and do nothing. In fact, they tend to support the bully instead of trying to stop the bully. This happens because it is not their responsibility to take control of the situation. That is the responsibility of the faculty and the administration. So they gather around and watch until some- one intervenes and stops the behavior. In the high performing school culture, students realize that they are supposed to take control of the situation and stop that kind of behavior. In this type of control culture, the peer group becomes a positive force. In chapter 5, we will describe "social contracting" as a way to decrease bullying and other forms of misbehavior.

DOES THE HIGH-PERFORMING CONCEPT REALLY WORK?

While the above statements are based on observations and opinion, are there data that support the belief that they really work? How difficult is it to implement the high-performing concept in a classroom or school? To answer these questions, an experiment was designed where 30 graduate students in educational leadership classes agreed to try it with their own students. One limitation was that it was implemented at **the classroom level** and not at the school level. The research design was as follows:

- Each graduate student was a teacher in a public school setting.
- Each graduate student counted for five weeks the number of redirects for their students. At the end of the five-week period, they calculated the aver- age number of redirects per day and/or week.
- Students were not told that they were part of an experiment.
- At the end of five weeks, the students were told of the average number of redirects and asked to help the teacher lower the average number. If they were successful, the entire class would receive a reward.
- Students were asked to select a reward that would be a good motivator.

Results

The number of redirects for students in each graduate student's classroom was reduced by more than 50 percent. A description of how the high-performing classroom concept worked in selected classrooms across the K–12 spectrum is as follows:

- In a kindergarten class, there was an average of 51 redirects per day for five weeks pre-experiment. During the five weeks post-experiment, there was an average of 13 redirects per day. To make the class aware of their progress regarding the number of redirects, cubes were added to a jar for good behavior, and cubes were removed for redirects. Students were rewarded when the jar was full.
- In a third grade class, there was an average of 20 redirects per week pre-experiment and an average of less than 10 redirects per week post-experiment.
- At a middle school in four classes, there was an average of 31 redirects per class per day and 585 per week pre-experiment compared to 13 redirects per day per class and 244 per week post-experiment.
- In a middle school emotional disorder class, there was average of 50 to 83 redirects per week pre-experiment compared to an average of 12 to 28 per week post-experiment. In commenting about what happened, the teacher wrote, "They were strongly motivated not to let each other down. I could not believe the improvement in their behavior. One week there was a sub, and they only got 28 violations. I could not believe they were able to keep it together."
- In a middle school physical education class, the redirects ranged from an average of 32 to 63 per week during the five weeks pre-experiment compared to 10 to 25 per week post-experiment.
- In a 10th grade English class, the average number of redirects was 35 per week and 7 per day pre-experiment and less than 1 per day post-experiment.
- A science teacher reported an average number of redirects of 60 per week for chemistry and 55 per week in biology pre-experiment and 25 per week in chemistry and 15 per week in biology post- experiment. This teacher commented that the students improved each week, and by the last week of the experiment, the chemistry class only had 10 redirects per week and the biology class only 8. In summarizing the results of the experiment, the teacher wrote, "My students have really taken charge of their behavior. I have seen outstanding results, and many teachers have commented on the change in my class."

In each of the above instances the students received a reward when the goal was reached. The selection of the reward is crucial. It has to be something they really want. Let them choose it, but give them some examples, such as free time on Friday, a pizza party, get rid of a low grade, being able to chew gum, recess, an open book test, homework passes, and so forth. If the high-performing concept is implemented at the classroom level, a weekly reward works best. If it is implemented at the school level, a daily or a weekly reward can be used. The best motivator is 5–10 extra minutes of locker time in the morning or 5–10 extra minutes prior to getting on the bus at the end of the day. Keep in mind that students can earn redirects during this extra 5–10 minutes.

Why does this work so well? According to Stetson, Hurley, and Miller (2003), "humans have two strong and conflicting desires: To become more autonomous, and to be connected to other humans" (p. 129). In a high-performing school, students have some feeling of control and ownership. Whether they get the reward is strictly up to them and the peer group.

The environment created by the high-performing school allows students to satisfy the two previously mentioned desires, but in this setting, they are not conflicting. They have a feeling of control (autonomy) because they under-stand what is expected of them, and they willingly choose to do the right thing, that is, moral power (discussed in chapter 4). The motivation is intrinsic, they are independent, they are empowered, and they are in control. At the same time, because the reward can only be achieved through a cooperative effort of the peer group, they have a connection with other students.

There is perhaps another reason why the high-performing school or class-room works so well. Joftus (2002), based on the research of others, stated that 40 percent of high school youth and 50 percent of middle school youth feel disengaged. Further, he stated that rates are even higher in urban and minor-ity schools. This leads to students simply giving up because they are bored, frustrated, and feel under appreciated. They feel that no one cares. In support of this opinion, Bulach, Fullbright, and Williams (2003) surveyed students on bullying behavior and found that 50 percent of them reported that, "people do not care about each other at our school." In a high-performing school or classroom, the peer group cares about the behavior of other students.

Since publication of the 1st edition of this book, four schools in Indiana have implemented Phase I where the control culture was shifted to students **at the school level**. Three elementary schools and one middle school imple-mented Phase I and the results were amazing. The number of teachers in the four schools was 114 and the number of students was 2175. The following procedures were used: Sometime during the first month of the school year and prior to implementing any part of the reform, each teacher in all four schools counted the number of times they had to correct or redirect each student's behavior for a week. Redirects were counted in the classroom, hallways, lunchroom, and other parts of the school.

- The teachers used clickers to count redirects for a week.
- After that week, the students were asked to help control each other's behavior; that is, control was shifted to students. Teachers did not give up control, but asked students to help control each other.
- Students were told that they would get extra recess time (elementary schools) or locker time (middle school) if they could reduce the number of times teachers had to control them or redirect student behavior.

They had an average of 2402 redirects a day during the pre-implementation week for all four schools. One teacher* had an average of 229 times a day she had to redirect students, while others had only 10–50/day. A great deal of time and effort was being exerted to control students. That was time taken away from teaching. The teacher with 229 redirects a day was averaging almost one redirect each minute. After 11 weeks of implementing the process, the number of redirects each day (post-implementation) was reduced to 595.

The existing culture, where the teachers were expected to control student behavior, was changed. The new culture was one where the students were being asked to control each others' behavior. It was now okay for students to control each other whereas in the past it was not legitimate for students to do that. For example, if students were misbehaving, one of the other students was expected to intervene and stop it. In most schools, students are not expected to intervene because that is the responsibility of the teachers and administrators.

What happened (post-experiment) was astounding! The students loved the new culture and went about controlling their own behavior and that of the other students with gusto. Every teacher reported a 50 percent or greater reduction in redirects. The teacher with 229 redirects **a day** (pre-experiment) averaged 35 a day after 11 weeks (85 percent reduction). One teacher, who averaged five redirects a day (pre-experiment), had zero (100 percent reduction) redirects a day (post-experiment).

All off task behaviors were reduced, resulting in greater time on task. The teachers at these four schools in September of 2009 stopped teaching to redirect students 2402 times a day. After 11 weeks of implementation of Phase I of the reform process, that dropped to 595 or a decrease of 76 percent. Once

---

*This was a special education teacher with a difficult class.

the new control culture becomes ingrained and students become more accustomed to controlling each other's behavior, there will be even fewer redirects. Implementing this process of shifting control to students at the school level creates a fundamental change in a school's culture and climate. Several principals reported that there were fewer office referrals as well.

The middle school that implemented the reform also collected pre-implementation data on school culture and climate and the character behavior of the students. We wanted to determine if the reform positively affected these two variables. A t-test (P <.05) for independent groups was the statistical analysis used to compare the pre-data from the spring of 2009 (pre-implementation) with the data from the spring of 2010 (post-implementation).

The overall mean on the school's culture and climate scores had improved significantly after one year of implementing the reform. The culture variable with the largest improvement was "group cooperation." The climate variables with the largest improvements were "discipline" and "sense of mission." A comparison of the character behavior scores pre- to post- did show an improvement but it was not statistically significant.

The data from the middle school supports the earlier findings of Bulach & Malone (1994) who also found a significant relationship between school climate and the implementation of a reform. Bulach (2006) in reporting on the character grant data in West Virginia found a significant relationship of $r = +.475$, $(p < .01)$ between culture/climate scores and character scores. A correlation of $+.57$ $(p <.05)$ was also found between the character data and student achievement.

In other research on these variables, Bulach (2006) looked at relationships between character scores and the individual culture and climate variables. The climate variable with the highest correlation with character scores $(+.577, p <.01)$ was parent involvement. Teacher expectations $(+.536, p <.01)$, followed by the way teachers teach $(+.532, p <.01)$ were the next highest correlations. The climate variable with the strongest relationship to all other culture and climate variables is the leadership of the principal. The leadership of the principal, with a correlation of $.476$ $(p <.05)$ also has a significant positive relationship with the character behavior of students. A significant relationship was also found between character behavior and the way discipline is administered $(+.490, p <.01)$.

Regarding comparisons of school culture and climate with student achievement, Bulach (2006) reported that they are positively related with correlations ranging from a low of $+.43$ to a high of $+.57$. In earlier research, Bulach & Malone (1995) found a positive correlation of $+.54$ with school climate and achievement. Based on the statistical data from previous research by Bulach, we can conclude that the variables of school culture, climate, character behavior of students, and student achievement are positively related. We also conclude that this school reform will improve school culture and climate with an eventual improvement in student achievement and students' character behavior. We hope to report that data in the 3rd edition of this book.

A few questions that could come to mind as you read this are the following: Does this change in the culture of control last? Why does it work? Do you have to teach students how to control each other? Should you allow students to control each other? What if students can't control each other? Based on past experience, I (Bulach) can state that this change in the culture of control will last indefinitely. Keep in mind that the idea for coming up with this change in the culture of control was the result of a middle school visitation in West Virginia. They had implemented a change in the control culture and were in their tenth year with the process. On the day of my visit, the teachers with a school population of 345 students had fewer than 25 times that they had to stop teaching to redirect students. Based on that experience, I think it can be stated that once the process is implemented, the change in the control culture will continue to be successful.

As for why it works, the answer is very simple: In most schools, the only people controlling behavior are the faculty. In this changed control culture, you have the faculty and all the students who are watching for behavior that needs redirecting. In the average classroom, instead of one pair of eyes (the teacher), you have 25 pairs of eyes (the students) plus the teacher, and that is why it is so effective in reducing off-task behavior.

The next question is "Do students have to be taught how to control each other?" The answer is a definite "No!" One needs only to think of "peer pressure" to understand that students are very capable of controlling each other when it is okay to control and they want to. Peer pressure is a very controlling force in any peer group. Within any school there are many different peer groups that exert control on their members. Changing the existing control culture creates a peer group for the whole school. All students are encouraged to help control each other and not just within their peer group.

Should you allow students to control each other? Isn't that what life is all about? Everyone is in control of something. We need to teach students how to control their life and those with whom they are involved. No one wants to be out of control and everyone wants to be in control. Allowing and encouraging students to control each others' behavior is what good citizens do. Imagine what would happen in Iraq if that had been taught. The splinter group of suicide bombers (bullies) would not be tolerated. They would be reported to authorities before someone got killed. However, because the control culture in that society it is not the responsibility of each individual. Instead they wait for someone else to deal with the problem. The same thing happens in our schools when students do what they are not supposed to do. They wait for faculty to correct the problem. In the school reform culture being described in this chapter, students will not wait on faculty. They will realize that it is each student's responsibility to step to the plate.

Regarding the question of what happens when a student refuses to be controlled by a peer? That does happen! There are students who will not allow other students to control their behavior. Some students are so anti-social that they continue to be disruptive no matter what their peers say or do to them. If that happens, teachers should not count redirects for that student and should not encourage the peer group to control that student.

Earlier, it was mentioned that this reform process should also reduce teacher absenteeism. Teacher absenteeism on Mondays and Fridays is much higher on these two days than the other days of the week. There are days when there are so many teachers absent on a Monday or a Friday that it is difficult to find a substitute because all the substitute teachers have already been hired.

Stress is the reason why teachers have such a high rate of absenteeism in general and why absenteeism is higher on Monday and Friday. The more stress teachers experience the higher the absenteeism rate. What causes stress? There are many factors: demands from the administration, declining test scores, disagreements with other faculty members, and so forth. However, one of the leading causes of stress is the need to control the students. It is not uncommon for a teacher to have to correct students 150 times a day or as in the case above, 229 times. That means that a teacher has to stop teaching and correct a student every two to three minutes. Having to stop teaching, correct a student, and restart teaching is a lot of stress.

This constant interruption of the learning process, whether caused by students' misbehavior or other interruptions, also reduces test scores leading to even greater stress and teacher absenteeism. By the time Friday roles around, some teachers have had all they can take, so they are absent. Come Monday, some teachers don't want to go back to work because they are mentally just not able, so they stay home another day.

In summary, the data at the classroom and school level prove that educators can give control to students without giving up control. Teachers who had to stop teaching a number of times found that they could teach almost without interruption. The culture of control in each classroom and the entire school can be changed. Students will control each other, not only in the classroom, but in the bathrooms, hallways, lunchroom, and so on. Earlier, it was mentioned that this creates a high performing school. Another word could be used. It could be called a "Citizenship" school, because in this school culture students help each other. If a student does not have a pencil, a book, their homework, or other classroom supplies, they help each other. It is human nature that people like to help each other. Change the existing control culture, and students will have many opportunities to practice good citizenship. A good citizen will not tolerate bullying behavior. They will not continue to be bystanders waiting for an adult to intervene.

How big a problem is bullying behavior? Last year (2009), the Departments of Education and Health and Human Services joined forces with four other departments to create a federal task force on bullying. In August 2010, the task force staged the first-ever National Bullying Summit, bringing together 150 top state, local, civic, and corporate leaders to begin mapping out a national plan to end bullying. The task force also launched a new website, www.bullyinginfo.org, which brings all the federal resources on bullying together in one place for the first time ever. A person who is being bullied or harassed can go to this site to find resources for help.

Additionally, Michelle Obama wrote in an October 23, 2010, e-mail, "Middle school and high school can be tough for any kid. But it can be especially wrenching if you're taunted or harassed by your peers, if you are made to feel worthless or alone because you don't look or act like everybody else. And if you're in that situation, it can be hard to imagine that things will ever change. But they will". It is very clear from the above messages that bullying behavior is a problem in our society and schools. If this school reform will positively impact bullying behavior (yet to be proven), and we believe it will because good citizens step to the plate and do not continue to be bystanders.

A good citizen does not rely on others, such as police, fire department, or school officials, to deal with a problem. They know that it is their responsibility to intervene, and if they can't deal with the problem, they call on a higher authority. In most schools today, they stand by and watch to see what the higher authority will do. I (Bulach) know this is what happens. While interviewing students in every school district in West Virginia, there was often a student who "acted out." The other students did nothing to this student who was "acting out." They wanted to see how I was going to "handle it." In the high performing school described in this chapter, the students would have handled it.

SUGGESTED PLAN FOR PHASE 1

There should be a weekly or daily reward for staying under the targeted number of redirects, or reminders. This is the peer group's motivator, and this can be done by classroom, team, grade level, or the whole school. There should also be an end-of-report–period reward for all students who have stayed under the targeted number of violations. This is the individual's motivator. There should be an individual daily punishment for anyone who exceeds a set number of redirects. There should be some way for students to redeem themselves if they have lost the privilege of taking part in the end-of-report-period reward.

This creates a two-pronged approach for shaping desirable student behavior as follows: (a) each student is encouraged to control their own behavior so they can eat lunch with their friends and participate in the end-of-report-period reward, and (b) they are encouraged to work with other students to receive the peer group reward. The result is a plan to reward desirable behavior and extinguish undesirable behavior. For those opposed to giving rewards because they feel students should do what they are supposed to do because it is the right thing to do and not because there is a reward, this process complies with reward theory. The reward is intermittent because it occurs at the end of the report period for those (the individual motivator) that earned it, and it is received by a group of students (the peer motivator). Students do not receive a reward each time they do something they are supposed to do.

Implementation of Phase 1 should occur at the school level, but if school officials want to try a gradual approach, they could ask some teachers to try it in their individual classrooms. Another alternative would be to start with office referrals, tardies, or absences or any combination of these. School officials should establish the benchmark and have a clearly visible indicator of progress toward achieving that benchmark. One such indicator is a thermometer-like poster near the entrance. Everyone in the school is aware of the progress or lack thereof in reaching the established mark for the group reward. If the benchmark is not exceeded, the entire school gets the reward. Whether the weekly or daily approach is used can be determined by school officials. However, we believe the daily benchmark for redirects is the most effective approach.

The role of all faculty should also be considered! We suggest that you involve the cooks, custodial staff, secretaries, and all other non-certified staff in the counting of redirects process. Whether and when to involve the bus drivers is a judgment call, but eventually, we believe they should also be involved. Another judgment call is when to use failure to do homework as a redirect. However, when to involve all non-certified is critical. They need to feel a part of the team and this is the easiest way to do it. Let them count redirects and they will know that they are just as important as the teachers and administration when it comes to having a role in improving student behavior.

CONCLUSION

There is a strong need to move away from using letter grades and punish-ment as motivators, as is the practice in traditional schools. A transition to enlightened traditional schools will be beneficial and is necessary in improv-ing the educational environment in today's institutions; however, changing the control culture creates a fundamental change in what happens at a school. In enlightened traditional schools, it is every individual for themselves. Each individual accrues their own rewards, creating a great deal of competition.

In the high-performing school culture, the reward goes to a group of stu-dents, creating cooperation. The end result tends to be a community where people work together as citizens for a common reward. A culture and climate that are absolutely wonderful are created. It is a collaborative environment where faculty and students work together. In his research, Gruenert (2005) concluded that a collaborative culture is the best setting for student achieve-ment. He warned that school leaders should not "lose sight of the bigger picture of creating the social conditions necessary for student and teacher success" (p. 51). A positive culture of control is created, and at the same time, a character education program that requires no curriculum or extra effort on the part of the faculty is in place. The high-performing school culture creates an environment where students and faculty have an opportunity to model responsibility, dependability, accountability, perseverance, courtesy, kind-ness, compassion, respect, cooperation, and tolerance.

In the traditional school, which represents most schools, there are few opportunities for students to practice good citizenship because they are being controlled by the administration and faculty. They are told what the rules and consequences are, and they must comply or face reprimand. In the enlight-ened traditional school, they are encouraged to control themselves, but it is a highly competitive environment. There is no incentive to help each other.

Many schools are the antithesis of what is required for the future of a successful society. Graduates are needed who have had opportunities to help each other, who have had experience working in a community of other citizens, who believe that they make a collective difference, who have expe-rienced the rewards of working together, and who are willing to step forward and intervene when needed. This does not occur in the traditional or enlight-ened traditional school.

Many opportunities for this to occur are present every day in a high-performing school culture. If we want good citizens, we must change the control culture that exists in most schools and create an environment that is more representative of what is expected when they graduate. We expect them to vote, we expect them to play an active role in their community, we expect them to be good parents (to serve their spouse and children), and we expect them to step forward when they see something that is wrong. If we maintain these expectations, we must create opportunities for them to practice these behaviors in the school setting.

There is more to school than academics. It should be a cocoon for creating citizens who are concerned not only for their own welfare, but for the welfare of the rest of the society in which they live. We need to graduate students who are servant leaders as opposed to self-serving. That is not occurring, as evidenced by a high dropout rate and the number of citizens who are actively involved in the political process, with only 50 percent of Americans stepping out to vote. While the concept of a high-performing school does work, it is even more effective if the entire faculty comes across as servant leaders and not as self-serving, and that is the subject of the next chapter.

REFERENCES

Beane, A. L. (2009). *Bullying prevention for schools: A step by step guide for implementing a successful anti-bullying program.* San Francisco: Jossey Boss.

Beane, A.L. & Bulach, C. R. (September, 2009). Tips for helping children who are bullied. *School Climate Matters.* The Center for Social and Emotional Education.

Berger, R. (2003). *An ethic of excellence: Building a culture of craftsmanship with students.* Portsmouth, NH: Heineman

Bulach, C. R., & Malone, B. (1994). The relationship of school climate to the implementation of school reform. *ERS SPECTRUM: Journal of School Research and Information* 12(4), 3–9.

Bulach, C. R., Malone, B., & Castleman, C. (1995). An investigation of variables related to student achievement. *Mid-Western Educational Researcher,* 8(2), 23–29.

Bulach, C. R., Fullbright, P. J., & Williams, R. (2003). Bullying behavior: What is the potential for violence at your school? *Journal of Instructional Psychology,* 30, 156–164.

Bulach, C. R., "An Analysis of the West Virginia Character Education Initiative." A presentation at the Character Education Partnership 13th National Forum on 10-27-2006 at Arlington, VA.

Gruenert, S. (2005). Correlations of collaborative cultures with student achievement. *NASSP Bulletin,* 89(645), 43–55.

Joftus, S. (2002, September). *The challenge: Academic failure among secondary students. Every Child A Graduate.* Washington, D.C.: Alliance for Excellent Education.

Kohn, A. (2006). *Beyond discipline : From compliance to community.* Alexandria, VA: Assn for Supervision & Curriculum, Development.

Kohn, A. (2004). Rebuilding school culture to make schools safer. *The Educational Digest,* 70(3), 23–30.

Marzano, R. J., Marzano, J. S., & Pickering, D. J. (2003). *Classroom management that works: Research-based strategies for every teacher.* Alexandria, VA: Association for Supervision and Curriculum Development.

Sergiovanni, T., & Starratt, R. (2002). *Supervision: A redefinition* (7th ed.). New York: McGraw-Hill.

Silva, P., & Mackin, R. A. (2002). *Standards of mind and heart: Creating the good high school.* New York: Teachers College Press.

Stetson, E. A., Hurley, A. M., & Miller, G. E. (2003). Can universal affective education programs be used to promote empathy in elementary children? *Journal of Research in Character Education*, 1(2), 129–147.

Chapter 2

A Four-Step Process for Identifying and Reshaping the Culture of a School

Phase Two

In chapter 1 we described Phase I for implementing a school reform. However, implementing a change in the control culture is only one phase for this comprehensive reform. Creating a high-performing culture distinctly different from that in most schools also requires an alternative kind of leadership, both for administrators and teachers. The leadership style needed for implementing this type of school culture has been described by Greenleaf (2008) and Blanchard and Hodges (2003) as servant leadership. In addition to implementing Phase 1 of the process it is also necessary to identify and reshape the existing culture of the school (Phase 2). First we will describe what is meant by servant leadership and the need for a comprehensive reform. Then we will describe each of the four steps for identifying and reshaping a school's existing culture.

SERVANT LEADERSHIP

Greenleaf is the founder of the Servant as Leader concept. His original 1970 work is a series of essays. The Robert K. Greenleaf Center was founded in 1985 to promote the servant leadership concept. In a 1991 publication (published posthumously in 1990), he wrote that a true leader must first become a servant. A leader who is a servant realizes that his or her first priority is the needs of the people being led. Keep in mind, however, that the needs of the organization must also be met.

An analogy of the apple tree can be used to illustrate this point. Think of the tree as the organization and the apples as the people. There can be no apples without the tree. This is also true of most organizations. If the

27

organization is not productive, it will not survive, and the staff will be job-less. A servant leader has to keep the needs of both in balance to maintain a high-performing school.

A principal must always balance the needs of the people (staff and students) and the needs of the organization (tasks and goals). Principals see this clearly as they accommodate teacher requests for teaching assignments, planning periods, and classroom assignments. The tasks must meet the needs of the organization—not all teachers can have the last period for planning or teach advanced placement classes. This is an example of the balls the principals must juggle in meeting the needs of the staff and the organization. However, this can create a problem for principals. In meeting the needs of the organization, the principal can appear self-serving. In this book, the authors show how to be a servant leader while at the same time meeting the needs of the staff and the organization.

A servant leader, through the creative use of power and authority, (the subject of chapter 4) creates a culture where there is a feeling of community and openness, trust, and cooperation. There should be opportunities for students and faculty to assume responsibility and improve personal abilities.

Greenleaf's (1996) ideas about leadership are expanded on by Blanchard and Hodges (2003). They take Greenleaf's concept and use the life of Jesus Christ to describe servant leadership. They maintain that he was a great leader because he came to serve. They stated that, "In his instructions to his disciples on how they were to lead, Jesus sent a clear message to all those who would follow Him that leadership was to be first and foremost an act of service" (p. 12). Lest the reader reject the concept of servant leadership because of their beliefs and the mention here of Jesus Christ, please keep in mind some of Blanchard's and Hodges's other thoughts on leadership.

They maintain that our public leadership style determines whether others will follow. If followers perceive that the leader's behavior and habits are self-serving, as opposed to the benefit of those who are being led, there will be resistance to that person's leadership. They maintain that many leaders are self-serving and addicted to power and recognition.

The concept of servant leadership has been around for more than 30 years, yet it has received little attention from most educational leaders. Is it possible that most leaders are self-serving and more concerned for their own welfare than for the people in the organization they are leading? According to Blanchard and Hodges (2003), "The reality is that we are all self-serving to a degree because we came into this world with self-serving hearts" (p. 22).

Is this why there is so much resistance to change and reform in education? Is this why improving the quality of instruction and improving test scores is so difficult? Is this why the No Child Left Behind law was passed? Greenleaf (1996) discussed and explained the role of listening, caring, trust, and the appropriate use of power and authority for servant leadership. However, they do not give a clear vision of how to operationalize the concept and create such a culture.

Such a culture is required for a high-performing school. In a high-performing school, servant leadership is practiced, not only by the principal, but also by the teachers and students. For example, the principal shares his or her power and authority with the teachers, and the teachers share the same with their students. This creates a culture where everyone has maximum opportunities to grow, mature, and become responsible, not because someone is supervising them, but because it is the right thing to do.

The end result is a school culture where all faculty, students, and parents are focused on being of service to each other. How can such a culture be created? In part I and chapters 1 through 5, the authors explain four distinct phases for creating such a culture. Any of these phases can help create such a culture, but when all four phases are implemented, a high-performing school, dedicated to the service of others, is more likely to occur. In chapter 2, we describe Phase 2 of the process. Creating a culture for a high-performing school will address the concerns of many critics of today's educational system.

THE NEED FOR A COMPREHENSIVE SCHOOL REFORM

Quint (2006) summarized lessons learned from three models of school reform and discussed the importance of caring learning communities for students. One of the findings is that many schools are too large and must be broken up into smaller learning communities so students will feel that their teachers know and care about them. Quint also discussed the need for and difficulty of a comprehensive school reform and the resistance to change.

The most recent report by the National Center on Education and the Economy (2007) also called for a comprehensive school reform. The report stated that there is a growing mismatch between the type of students our schools are producing and the needs of the economy. The report detailed a series of initiatives designed to reform the way schools operate.

According to Marc Tucker, vice chairman of the center and architect of the report, "This country is cooked if we don't make a vast improvement in the outcomes for our kids" (Olszewski & Rado, 2006, p. 10A). The resistance to this initiative/change has already been expressed by Antonia Cortese, the executive vice president of the American Federation of Teachers. She stated that the proposal contained "some seriously flawed ideas with faddish allure that won't produce better academic results" (Herszenhorn, 2006, p. A9).

While the New Commission's report is the most recent, there are many other reports that have called for school reform. For example, the National Governors Association hosted an unprecedented two-day National Education Summit on High Schools in 2005. It was attended by 45 governors, educators, and business leaders. The purpose of the summit was to address the nation's alarming dropout rate and the fact that most students leave high school without the skills necessary for success in college or the workplace. In the opening session of the summit, Bill Gates stated that the nation's high schools were obsolete (Omear, 2005).

Steinberg, Johnson, and Pennington (2006), in a report for the Center for American Progress, wrote that it is time for an aggressive national effort to pursue a high school reform effort that addresses two needs: (a) a reduction in the dropout rate and (b) higher standards. According to the report, one-third of all high school students do not graduate. Allowing more than 1 million students a year to drop out without a diploma is too great a cost. Further, according to the report, the federal government needs to pass a Graduation Promise Act that would fund the implementation of proven strategies for keeping students in school and improving student achievement.

The Koret Task Force (2003) also reaffirmed the lack of progress in school reform. Further, according to the Time magazine cover article "Dropout Nation" (Thornburgh, 2006) and the follow-up Oprah Winfrey poll, "55 percent of Americans are dissatisfied with public schools and 61 percent think public schools are in a crisis" (Amos, 2006, p.3). Boone, Hartzman, and Mero (2006), in trying to address the need for reform, wrote "Breakthrough High Schools: Lessons Learned." However, a specific plan on how to create such a school was not given. Clearly it is time to come up with a school reform that will address this need and reduce resistance to change.

Chapter 1 describes one of the four phases needed for a comprehensive approach to school reform. The remainder of this chapter and chapters 3 through 5 are devoted to describing a clear process for creating a culture and climate for a high-performing or "Citizenship school." In parts II and III, the authors detail techniques, strategies, and processes for enhancing and maintaining that culture and climate.

HOW DOES OUR APPROACH ADDRESS THE NEED?

In this book, the authors unveil a comprehensive school reform approach that reduces resistance to school reform and increases the likelihood of creating a caring learning community. Creating a high-performing school is an organizational approach to school reform that creates a distinctly different school culture and climate than can be found in existing schools. Based on research (described in chapter 1), students like being part of such a culture. They have some control over their environment and are part of a caring learning community. This should result in a lower dropout rate and reduce bullying behavior. Further, the type of student produced by this school environment should be a more productive citizen. How can a school leader implement this approach without encountering resistance to this change?

Organizational theorists like Warren Bennis and others are aware that a leader who attempts a reform or change is in for a struggle because the system will resist the change. The secret for successful leadership is to identify the existing culture and reshape it to minimize the struggle. Principals who fail to identify the existing culture before introducing change will be met with resistance.

It is Bulach's belief, based on his 14 years as a superintendent, that a principal must identify the existing culture. If not, the odds are 50/50 that in two or three years, the system will win the struggle, and the principal will be searching for another job. Consequently, a major task in Phase 2 for creating the culture for a high-performing school is to identify and reshape the existing culture. According to Peterson and Deal (2002),

"Every principal should take some time to decipher the symbolic glue that holds a school together. The easiest time to do this is when the principal is new and not yet indoctrinated into existing mores and norms. But it can also be done by any veteran who makes the commitment." (p. 133)

Bulach (2001a) laid out a four-step process for doing this that also arranges the groundwork for the introduction of the servant leadership concept. The first step is to identify the existing culture described by Deal and Peterson (2009) as a set of expectations that affects the daily interactions of people and provides meaning and purpose for what happens in the work setting.

THE "EXPECTATIONS DIAGNOSIS: FACULTY INPUT (STEP 1)

While there are other techniques for identifying a school's culture, such as surveys and outside consultants, a technique Bulach calls "the expectations diagnosis" is preferred (Step 1). This technique requires little time and can be accomplished at the first faculty meeting of the school year. The expectations diagnosis requires that all faculty members receive three 3 × 5 index cards. They should write an expectation they have of the principal on each card. These expectations can be how they want to be treated and/or the rules they want enforced. Writing one expectation per card allows for easy sorting. More or less than three cards can be used, but based on past experience with this process, three cards works best. An explanation of why this information is needed and how it will be used should be made since trust has likely not been established.

The principal should explain to the faculty that one of the duties of the leader is to enforce rules and policies for both students and faculty. While the rules and policies for students tend to be clear, those for faculty are likely more flexible and subject to interpretation. Explain that their input on the rules and expectations is needed in order for the school to function at peak efficiency. Clarify how the 3 × 5 cards will be used and that one expectation per card allows them to be quickly sorted into common groups.

This input allows teachers' values and beliefs to be included in decisions that affect them, which is important for empowerment and in gaining trust with staff. Teachers who are empowered will feel that they have a voice in how the school operates, and there will be less disenchantment with policies and rules that affect them. Obviously, teachers can't decide things such as the pay scale or school calendar, but they can have a voice in school regulations such as dress-down day, staff parking, and so forth.

Once the cards are sorted into piles, it will be easy to identify the values, beliefs, or culture regarding the type of leadership the faculty prefers. A list of the 10 to 15 most frequently mentioned expectations should be compiled. This list is then given to faculty, and they are asked to rank items from most important to least important. Based on the rankings, the faculty's expectations regarding leadership can be determined. These expectations are shared with the faculty, and what was previously a hidden culture becomes a shared one.

What tends to emerge is a list of rules/expectations regarding faculty and administrator interactions. Research indicates that some likely rules/expectations are as follows:

- faculty should be involved in the decision-making process;
- all faculty should be treated the same;
- the principal must be consistent in disciplining students who are sent to the office;
- rules should be enforced;
- the principal should be visible; and
- the principal will work with individuals who violate rules of the school or district instead of berating the entire faculty at a staff meeting.

This process creates a subtle shift in power, as it puts the principal in the position of enforcing the expectations of the faculty rather than those of the principal. The principal is serving the faculty, and servant leadership is in place. For example, if a faculty member is routinely late for work, he or she is informed that the faculty expects the principal to enforce the rules, and one of those regulations is that they must be on duty at 7:30 a.m. Instead of having to use position, reward, and coercion power to enforce the rules, the principal can now use information and moral power.

Moral power is a term used by Sergiovanni and Starratt (2006) and Bulach (1999) to describe a form of power that motivates others to do what they are supposed to do because it is the right thing to do. The fact that the faculty has set the rules and expectations creates a very different power relationship. Moral power is a form of power that can never be used too often, whereas position power, if used too often, tends to lose its force. However, if moral power does not work, the principal must use position power to enforce the rules. The nine forms of power and their use and misuse are described in chapter 4.

There is no best way to conduct an expectations diagnosis. Some principals may prefer to set aside five to ten minutes at the start of the first faculty meeting. Others may want to collect expectations at the end of the day. A word of caution: We suggest that this should be done as a spontaneous expectations diagnosis, where teachers can think and respond independently. If they are allowed to get together and discuss it, the individual values and beliefs may not be identified.

Keep in mind that the rest of the staff, that is, custodians, paraprofessionals, cooks, bus drivers, and so forth, also have expectations that will shape the culture of the institution. The same process should be used with those individuals. It is suggested that different colored index cards be used to assist with the sorting process. Their expectations are likely to be different from those of the certified faculty. The colored cards allow each group's expectations to be identified.

According to Barth (2002), a leader cannot reshape a school's culture until the existing culture is identified. This process is the first step in identifying and reshaping the existing culture, and it initiates the concept of servant leadership. Reshaping the culture occurs because the leader has listened to the faculty/staff and laid the groundwork for the development of trust.

Greenleaf (1996) and Blanchard and Hodges (2003) have discussed the importance of listening for servant leadership. Greenleaf believes that the act of listening builds strength in others because their needs are being met when listening occurs. Listening is also an activity that conveys that the leader cares about the faculty's opinions, beliefs, and values. It also expresses that the leader is open to changing their leadership style to better meet faculty expectations.

Openness and trust are clearly intertwined (Bulach & Peterson, 1999). Once faculty perceive that the principal is there to serve their interests and that he or she cares and is open to them, the foundation for trust has been formed. The existing culture cannot be reshaped without some level of trust between the principal, faculty, and staff.

Gibb (1978) described the importance of openness and trust for high-performing organizations. He maintains that as trust grows, people become more open and less fearful, and change is more likely to occur. He stated that schools with high levels of trust will quickly outperform schools with low levels. He portrayed a school with low levels of trust as one where the principal comes in as an outsider and imposes his or her values on the faculty. This causes "a massive system defense that mobilizes counter energy. This defense mobilization is then interpreted by the well-intentioned official as corroborative of his or her disdain and distrust" (p. 198).

Once the school official decides that the faculty does not trust him or her, a more controlling form of leadership occurs that further mobilizes counter energy. This causes more controlling and more counter energy, and so the cycle of under performance continues until the leader is replaced. In schools where there are high levels of trust, the use of authority and controlling forms of power (discussed in chapter 4) are curtailed because faculty and students are self-determined and intrinsically motivated.

While the expectations diagnosis sets the stage for faculty to trust the leader, it also conveys to the faculty/staff that the leader trusts them. Step 1 creates a process for openness and allows subordinates to set the parameters for the operation of the school. Based on our experience with this process, the rules and expectations of the faculty are going to be more stringent than the rules that would be set by the administration. The principal in such a setting is in a much more powerful position than if s/he were enforcing the rules of the administration.

THE "EXPECTATIONS DIAGNOSIS: STUDENT INPUT (STEP 2)

Step 2 is the same process repeated by each teacher with their students. Students should be given three 3×5 index cards and asked to list three rules that should govern behavior in the classroom. This causes a dramatic change in the culture of the classroom because the teacher has become a servant. As a servant of the students, the teacher is enforcing the students' rules rather than the teacher's. Please note that the focus for students is "rules" whereas with faculty it was with "expectations."

Because there is only one rule on each card, they can quickly be sorted into common piles for identification purposes. A chart of the most frequently mentioned rules should be made. The chart should contain at least 10 rules. More can be added, but the more rules a teacher has the more difficult enforcement becomes. If a teacher wants a rule that the students have not identified, that rule can be included. The students will never know that the teacher put that rule on the chart. The use of redirects, described in chapter 1, can now be used by the teacher. If a rule is being broken by a student, the teacher should look at that student, and wait several seconds for the students to take charge or change that student's behavior. That wait time and look should not be counted as a redirect.

The psychological shift when students break their own rules versus those of the teacher is another example of moral power versus position power. The students set the rules for the right kind of behavior in the classroom. All the teacher has to do is remind students of how to do things right versus using position power to make students do the right thing. For example, if the classroom chart of rules is posted and a student is violating rule 2, the teacher only has to announce that rule 2 is being violated (a redirect). All eyes in the classroom focus on the student breaking that rule, and normally the student violating the rule will stop violating it.

There have been teachers in the Indiana schools who used the redirects as a hammer to control the students. They became even more control oriented than prior to implementing the redirects. The second they saw a student misbehaving, they called out "redirect." They did not give students a chance to correct their own behavior. That is an incorrect use of redirects. Teachers should give students a few seconds to correct their own behavior before counting a misbehavior as a redirect.

Marzano, Marzano, and Pickering (2008) described the importance of classroom management. Their research shows that there is a 28 percent reduction in classroom disruptions and a 20 percent increase in achievement when classroom rules and procedures are effectively implemented. If students are involved in setting the rules, they will help the teacher enforce the rules. The data from chapter 1 indicates that there can be a 70 percent or more reduction in redirects if students are given some control over their own behavior. Students like the feeling and belief that they have some control over what happens in a classroom as opposed to the traditional setting where enforcing rules and procedures is the sole responsibility of the teacher. The end result is a reduction in redirects, time off task, and an increase in student achievement.

By being open and listening to students, the teacher demonstrates that he or she cares about the students and lays the groundwork for trust to develop. According to Bulach, Brown, and Potter (1998) and Bulach (2001b), there are five sets of behaviors that create a caring learning environment. They are:

1. anxiety-reducing behaviors
2. listening behaviors

3. rewarding behaviors
4. recognition behaviors
5. friendship behaviors

The importance of listening behaviors was further described in Bulach (2000), where he wrote,

> The willingness to listen conveys that teachers are open to students. Students perceive that teachers care and this causes them to be open to their teachers. This is the foundation for trust to develop. Rapport between teachers and students is necessary before they take the risk of being open to learning.

The following paradigm (see Figure 2.1) is an illustration of how this process can work:

THE LEARNING PROCESS

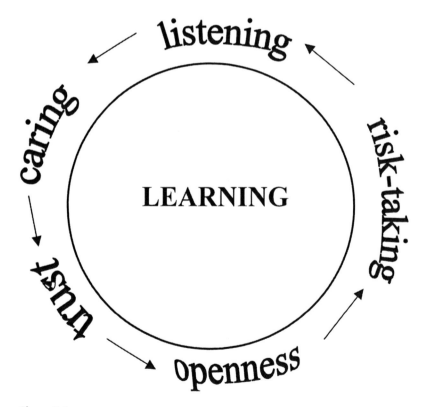

Figure 2.1

In order for learning to occur, the process begins with teachers showing students that they are willing to listen: This indicates to students that teachers care; students start trusting teachers, students are open and risk exposing themselves to the learning process. As students experience success, the cycle is repeated and students' motivation and learning increase. Granted there are other factors such as the teachers' personality, expertise, experience, subject content, etc., that are factors in the learning process. However, I believe that students will not risk learning until openness and trust are established. This basic human relationship between teachers and students starts with listening to students and showing them that you care." (p. 8)

The role of caring in creating a high performing school culture can't be emphasized enough. Berger (2003) stated that "Schools need to consciously shape their cultures to be places where it's safe to care, where it's cool to care." (p. 35) We believe that this feeling and belief that others care about you is a basic human need. Going back to Maslow's hierarchy of needs (1954), caring is essential for safety, belonging, and esteem needs if self actualization or learning is to occur.

GETTING FEEDBACK ON FACULTY AND STUDENT EXPECTATIONS (STEP 3)

Step 3 in reshaping culture is to find out how teachers and students are responding to the school's leadership and how they are making adjustments as needed. Using a technique made popular by Kurt Lewin (1951) called "force field analysis," there is a need to identify those forces "for" and "against" being the best possible principal or teacher. This should take place six to eight weeks after the start of the school year. It can actually take place at any time, so long as those responding have enough history to give a valid response. Use index cards or a sheet of paper, and have them complete the following two sentences as many times as they wish.

The principal is doing a good job because . . . (forces for)
The principal would do a better job if . . . (forces against)

This same force field analysis process should be repeated by each of the teachers in their respective classrooms. Each teacher should identify those forces for and against their being the best possible teacher.

(Name of teacher) is a good teacher because . . . (forces for)
(Name of teacher) would be a better teacher if . . . (forces against)

Again, this shows that the leader/teacher is willing to listen to faculty/students and is concerned about their welfare, cares about them, is willing to change the leadership style, and is there to serve. This allows the formation of trust to continue, and valid feedback on the faculty's perception of the principal's leadership will be received. Based on the feedback, the principal/teacher can build on strengths or address things s/he would like to change. Identifying problems early in the school year allows the principal and teachers to be proactive rather than reactive when the problems surface later in the year.

According to Blanchard and Hodges (2003), one of the quickest ways to spot a self-serving leader as opposed to a servant leader is the way they handle feedback. The self-serving leader usually responds negatively because they think their leadership is not wanted, or they will rationalize why they are truly doing a good job as principal. The servant leader, however, welcomes feedback as an opportunity to provide better service to his clients, that is, staff, students, parents, and the community.

A more formal approach for the principal to getting feedback and assessing their leadership is the Leadership Behavior survey. The survey measures behaviors in five areas that have allowed principals to create a positive supervisory climate or caused them to create a negative one (Bulach, Boothe, & Pickett, 2006). The five areas are the following: human relations, trust, instructional leadership, control, and conflict. Through the use of the inventory, faculty members describe their perception of how their principal practices 49 leadership behaviors* that have been identified as important for a positive supervisory climate. Based on the data, the principal can identify strengths and weaknesses in these five supervisory areas.

The concept of servant leadership and the creation of a culture for a high-performing school must permeate the school. The principal asking the teachers and the teachers asking the students "How am I doing?" demonstrates that the leaders care and are there to serve. The same process could be extended to the rest of the staff—secretaries, cafeteria workers, custodians, and so forth. This creates a culture of openness and risk-taking, both of which facilitate the development of trust (Bulach, 1974).

CULTURE AND CLIMATE DEFINED (STEP 4)

The final step is assessing the climate and culture of the school four to six weeks prior to the end of the school year. This can be done through a formal or an informal survey. If an informal survey is chosen, the same force field

---

*the behaviors associated with each of the five factors can be found at this website (www.westga. edu/~cbulach).

analysis process used to garner feedback on leadership style can be used. Two sentences faculty can complete as many times as they want are:

I like working at this school because . . .
I would like working at this school better if . . .

The same process could be used for students and parents, using a variation of the two sentences. For example, I like going to this school because and better if (students), or I like sending my child to school because and better if (parents).

If a formal survey is desired, an administrator's association, such as National Association of Secondary School Principals, National Association of Elementary School Principals, or American Association of School Administrators, can be contacted for information about surveys. There are a number of climate and culture surveys available. Another source for school climate surveys is the National Center for School Climate at http://www.schoolclimate.org/. Definitions of culture and climate differ widely, and in some cases are used synonymously. However, they are distinctly different. This difference can best be described by using the analogy of an iceberg.

Climate is the part of an iceberg that is easily seen above the water, and culture is the part of the iceberg below the water. The section below the water can't be seen, but it is there. The segment of the iceberg above the water can't exist without the part below the water. Similarly, the climate (what can be seen in a school) cannot exist without the underlying culture (what can't be seen). This is a causal relationship, that is, the underlying belief and value system (culture) causes the behavior that occurs in the organization (climate). Bulach, Malone, and Castleman (1995) described culture and climate as those psychological (culture) and institutional variables (climate) that give an organization its personality.

While there are instruments that measure culture or climate, it is difficult to find one that measures both organizational variables. One instrument* that measures both was used by Bulach, Berry, and Williams (2001). The culture variables are group openness, trust, cooperation, and atmosphere. This part of the survey provides data about how receptive people are, how trusting people are, how much individuals are willing to work together, and how much people care about one another. The climate variables are discipline, leadership, instruction, expectations, sense of mission, time on task/assessment, and parent involvement. These are also the "effective school" variables.** This

---

*Research manuscripts and reports where the culture and climate survey and the leadership behavior survey mentioned in this chapter were used can be viewed and accessed at www.westga.edu/~cbulach.

**Association for Effective Schools (http://www.mes.org/correlates.html)

part of the survey provides data on the extent to which students obey rules, if the principal leads, how teachers teach, and so forth.

The advantage of the formal survey is that it provides detailed information about a school's strengths and areas needing improvement. The data are quantitative and allow for comparisons of pre- and post-data to measure the effectiveness of the school improvement plan. The use of an outside consultant to generate the climate/culture profile also adds authenticity to the data. The disadvantage is that there are costs involved for surveys, computer scan forms, data analysis, and writing of the report.

The advantage of the informal survey is that it is quick, easy, and costs only the time needed to analyze and describe the data. Since the data are of a qualitative nature, it is more difficult to analyze and make comparisons to see if the culture and climate has improved as a result of the improvement plan. One method of measuring the effectiveness of the plan, when qualitative data are used, is to count the number of times the faculty identify something they like about the school (forces for) and the number of times they identify something that would cause them to like the school better (forces against). If the plan has worked, the post–school improvement plan data should have an increase in the number of things they liked (forces for) about the school and a decrease in the number of items they did not like (forces against).

CONCLUSION

School principals must identify the existing culture if they wish to introduce the servant leadership approach. They also have to change the culture that operates in most classrooms. This can happen if leaders and teachers become more servant leadership-oriented. They must create conditions where the followers/subordinates create the rules and policies and the leader enforces them. The faculty and students identify the culture they want in the school, and the principal and teachers help create and reshape it into a healthy learning environment. This continues the process of changing the control culture described in chapter 1.

Receiving early feedback on the supervisory climate created by the administration and teachers is important in avoiding more serious problems that could occur waiting for end-of-year feedback. The overall culture and climate that have been created in the school also need to be analyzed and a plan implemented to improve it (the subject of chapter 3). These are proactive techniques that allow the reshaping of the culture and climate of a school where both the needs of the organization and the people within the organization are being met.

While the above process describes a plan for principals to use in identifying and reshaping the culture and climate of a school, the same process can be used by school superintendents and other administrators. The expectations of board members, teachers, and the administrative team can be ascertained using the same process. The supervisory climate of the superintendent can also be measured.

While the concept of servant leadership can exist at the building level and not at the district level, it would be fascinating to see what would happen if all central office and building personnel implemented in Phase 1 and Phase 2 the groundwork for high-performing schools. Last, but not least, superintendents who ignore the climate and culture of the schools in their district are ignoring early indicators of schools that are headed for a decline in student achievement scores.

The call for school reform grows stronger with each report released, like the findings of the National Center on Education and the Economy. It is time for a new approach, and we believe the methods outlined in this and other chapters will be beneficial for educators and will produce students who complete high school and become productive citizens.

REFERENCES

Amos, J. (2006). Oprah's on!: Oprah Winfrey, Bill and Melinda Gates, and more than 50 other partners announce national campaign on high school dropouts. *Alliance for Education*: Straight A's, 6(8), 2–4.

Barth, R. (2002). The culture builder. *Educational Leadership*, 59(8). 6–11.

Berger, R. (2003). *An ethic of excellence: Building a culture of craftsmanship with students*. Portsmouth, NH: Heineman.

Blanchard, K., & Hodges, P. (2003). *The Servant Leader*. Nashville, TN: J. Countryman.

Boone, E., Hartzman, M., & Mero, D. (2006). Breakthrough high schools: Lessons learned. *Principal Leadership*, 6(10), 51.

Bulach, C. R. (1974). The relationship of openness, trust, and risk-taking. Doctorial dissertation, University of Cincinnati, Cincinnati, Ohio.

Bulach C. R. (1999). Leadership techniques that control or empower subordinates: A new power typology. Presentation at the Southern Regional Council of Education Administration, Charlotte, North Carolina, November 15, 1999.

Bulach, C. R. (2000). How to show your TESOL students that you care! *TESOL in Action*, 14(1), 7–9.

Bulach, C. R. (2001a). A four-step process for identifying and reshaping school culture. *Principal Leadership*, 1(8), 48–51.

Bulach, C. R. (2001b). Now more than ever: Show kids you care! *The Education Digest*, 67,(3), 4–7.

Bulach, C. R., & Peterson, T. A. (2001, November). Analyzing levels of openness and trust between principals and their teachers. *SRCEA 2001 Yearbook: Leadership for the 21st Century*.

Bulach, C. R., Berry, J., & Williams R. (2001). The impact of demographic factors on school culture and climate. Paper presented at the Southern Regional Council of Educational Administrators, Jacksonville, Florida, November 3, 2001.

Bulach, C. R., Boothe, D., & Pickett, W. (2006). Analyzing the Leadership Behavior of School Principals. CONNEXIONS. Retrieved October 25, 2006 from, www.cnx.org/content/m13813/latest.

Bulach, C. R., Brown, C., & Potter, L. (1998). Behaviors that create a caring learning community. *Journal of a Just and Caring Education*, 4(4), 458–470.

Bulach, C. R., Malone, B., & Castleman, C. (1995). An investigation of variables related to student achievement. *Mid-Western Educational Researcher*, 8(2), 23–29.

Deal T. E., & Peterson, K. D. (2009). *Shaping school culture: Pitfalls, paradoxes, and promises*. San Francisco : Jossey-Bass.

Gibb, J. R. (1978). *TRUST: A new view of personal and organizational development*. Los Angeles: Guild of Tutors Press.

Greenleaf, R. K. (1996). *On becoming a Servant Leader*. Somerset, NJ: John Wiley & Sons Inc.

Herszenhorn, D. M. (2006, December 12). Back to drawing board on education? *Atlanta Journal-Constitution*, p. A9.

Koret Task Force. (2003). *Are we still at risk*. Palo Alto, CA: Hoover Institute.

Lewin, K. (1951). *Field theory in social sciences*. New York: Harper & Row.

Maslow, A (1954). *Motivation and personality*. New York: Harper and Row.

Marzano, R. J., Marzano, J. S., & Pickering, D. J. (2008). *Classroom management that works: Research based strategies for every teacher*. Lebanon, IN: Merrill.

National Center on Education and the Economy. (2007). *Tough choices or tough times: The report of the new commission on the skills of the American workforce*. San Francisco: John Wiley & Sons.

Olszewski, L., & Rado, D. (2006, December 15). Panel calls for radical reform of U.S. education. *The Chicago Tribune*, p. 10A.

Omear, J. (2005, February). Leaders call for equity, rigor in the American high school. News Release From the National Governors Association. Retrieved October 25, 2006 from, http://www.nga.org/portal/site/nga/menuitem.6c9a8a9ebc6 ae07eee28aca9501010a0/?vgnextoid=185f137945da2010VgnVCM1000001a0101 0aRCRD&vgnextchannel=759b8f2005361010VgnVCM1000001a01010aRCRD.

Peterson, K. D., & Deal, T. E. (2002). *The shaping school culture fieldbook*. San Francisco: Jossey-Bass.

Quint, J. (2006). Research-based lesson for high school reform: Findings from three models. *Principals Research Review*, 1(3), 1–8.

Sergiovanni, T., & Starratt, R. (2006). *Supervision: A redefinition* (8th ed.). New York: McGraw-Hill.

Steinberg, A., Johnson, C., & Pennington, H. (2006). *Addressing America's dropout challenge: State efforts to boost graduation rates require federal support.* Washington, D.C.: Center for American Progress.

Thornburgh, N. (April, 2006). Dropout nation. *Time Magazine*, 167(16), 31–40.

Chapter 3

Implementing a Plan to Improve the Climate and Culture of the School

Phase Two Continued

The control culture and the system of redirects should be firmly established by this time. The groundwork should have been laid for improving the culture of the school, and servant leadership should be in place at the school and classroom level. The values and beliefs of the teachers and students governing human interactions should have been identified through the "expectations diagnosis." Administrators and teachers should have received feedback on how their leadership is being accepted by subordinates. According to Danielson (2002), a culture of respect and responsiveness for clients is very important if school improvement is to take place.

The four-step process for identifying and reshaping the culture of a school demonstrated to faculty and students that the leaders care and consider them important. Administrators and faculty are still very much in control, but control has been shifted to faculty and students. Remember the earlier statement in chapter 1: People want to be in a highly controlled environment, but still want to have some control. A lack of control is something no one likes to feel.

The final step the authors describe in chapter 2 is collecting data on the culture and climate of the school. This is necessary in developing a school improvement plan for the next school year. The principal needs to explain to the faculty that the mission of the school is to improve the quality of instruction and create a caring learning environment. How the faculty will be involved in using this data to create a vision to accomplish this mission is crucial in continuing to reshape school culture. In this chapter, the authors explain how the faculty can be involved; how to analyze and utilize the data; and how to compare data before and after the school improvement plan.

Stolp and Smith (1995) discussed the principal's role in creating a vision for his or her school. They maintained that the principal should be a facilitator in the process and should not impose his/her own beliefs on the faculty. This opinion is shared by others who have also written extensively on creating a vision for a positive organizational culture (Cunningham & Gresso, 1993; Fullan, 2009; Senge, 1990).

According to Stolp and Smith (1995), the characteristics of such a culture are as follows:

> The organization's members must listen to one another, feel empowered to change the organization, have confidence in their ability to improve their performance, think critically and gather data about where the organization is at present, and hold strong convictions about the ideals that should guide their work in the future. (p. 69)

DECIDING HOW TO PROCEED

In the first part of Phase 1, control is shifted to faculty and students and conditions are created for improving levels of trust between the administration and teachers and for a positive organizational culture to develop. If levels of trust are to continue improving, teachers have to be involved in developing the improvement plan. According to King (2002), the role of principals has changed. Principals must develop the leadership capacity of teachers by involving them in the decision-making process, and they must provide opportunities for them to collaborate on school improvement issues. According to Berger (2003), teachers on many school staffs feel no ownership beyond their classroom and they feel powerless to deal with the broad issues of school culture. That has to change and the way the school is organized should be determined by the faculty and not the principal.

Teacher involvement in shaping a school's culture is often determined by how the school is organized. Danielson (2002), also agrees with Berger and wrote, "How a school is organized is a matter for the staff to determine, and a school's organization should reflect the staff's commitment to the success of all students" (p. 43). Granted, all schools have some pre-existing organizational pattern, and this is a good time to involve the faculty and ask if the pre-existing pattern can be improved. If teams, departments, houses, or any other pattern are used to organize the school, it is time to gather feedback on that organization. The "force field analysis" technique described by the authors in chapter 2 can be used as follows (complete the following two sentences as often as you wish):

> The structure of organizing this school by (describe here—is it by grade level teams, departments, etc.) is good because . . .
> The structure of organizing this school by (describe here) would be better if . . .

The next step is to appoint a committee to analyze the data on the culture and climate (chapter 2) and on the organizational structure. Keep in mind that the formation of a committee could have been done much earlier. When the committee is appointed is not crucial; however, how the committee is appointed is very important if the trust-building process is to continue.

APPOINTING THE COMMITTEE

The committee should consist of representatives from each group of the preexisting organizational structure. Care should be taken to ensure that all members of the faculty are represented by the committee. This includes both certified and non-certified faculty. If trust building is to continue, it is imperative that the faculty be allowed to decide who will represent their group on the committee. If the principal appoints members, this will come across as self serving, and it is a clear signal to the faculty that he or she does not trust them.

According to Stolp and Smith (1995), culture building "is a process that cuts deeply into the fabric of people's relationships, their patterns of communication and interaction, and their regard for their own potential as well as that of the organization they serve. An excellent culture is the net result of the activities of individuals who are themselves, both on their own and as members of a work group, growing in identity, confidence, knowledge, cooperation, commitment, and respect." (p. 64)

In keeping with that philosophy, the principal must allow the faculty to select their own representatives and elect the chair. The principal should serve as a facilitator and non-voting member. The principal also has to dictate what the committee's role will be in the culture improvement process. Will the committee have the authority to make decisions or only recommendations? If they only have the authority to make recommendations to the principal or site-based council, it should be made very clear. If they have the authority to make decisions, is that authority limited to the school improvement plan? It is important that the members of the committee understand their role.

The first task of the committee is to elect a chair. The second task is to decide how decisions will be made. Will they be made by majority vote or consensus? If by consensus, the committee must decide what is meant by consensus. There are different levels of consensus ranging from "I have some reservations, but I will support the decision" to "I wholeheartedly agree with and support the decision." Getting everyone to agree could be very time consuming. A lower level of consensus might be more advisable.

The next task is to analyze the force field analysis data on the school's preexisting organizational structure. If the forces for or against indicate a need to change the organizational structure, the committee should review those forces and make the necessary recommendations or decisions. According to Marzano (2003), the governance or organizational structure is crucial for high-performing schools. Also according to Lunenburg and Ornstein (2008), the organizational structure should be such that all personnel in the school are included in some group, allowing for a communication network where there are no "isolates." An "isolate" is a person who is not connected to another person in the school organizational structure.

If all personnel in the school are connected to some group (no isolates), then everyone is in the communication loop, allowing all personnel to have input in the communication process. If, as a result of the committee's recommendation, the organizational structure is revised and new groups are created, the school-improvement committee should be expanded to include a representative from those groups. Once the committee is intact, has chosen a leader, and has reached consensus on how decisions will be made, the process of analyzing the culture and climate data collected in chapter 2 can begin.

ANALYZING THE DATA

In this section the authors describe two different ways to view the data. One method is to look at data from a quantitative standpoint. This method assumes that a formal survey was used to collect the data. The other method looks at data from a qualitative standpoint and assumes that an informal survey was used to gather the data. Hopefully, the quantitative data have been depicted in a bar graph, and based on the scores; it is easy to identify the strengths and areas needing improvement. For example, if the Bulach (2002) Instructional Improvement Survey (IIS) were used, there will be scores (see Appendix A) for the four culture variables (group openness, trust, cooperation, and atmosphere), and scores for the seven climate variables (discipline, teaching, instructional leadership, expectations, sense of mission, assessment/time on task, and parent involvement).

The scores represented on the graph are the result of faculty responses to the behaviors that make up each of the four culture and seven climate variables (this graph compares scores from the previous year with changes in the current year's scores as a result of the school improvement plan). Scores near or above 32 indicate areas of strength and those below areas that should be considered for improvement. Each variable or subscale is measured by eight (8) behaviors. An agree response is scored as a four (4), which would produce a score of 32 ($4 \times 8 = 32$). A disagree response is scored as a two (2), which would produce a score of 16 ($2 \times 8 = 16$). A completely agree response is scored as a five (5) producing a score of 40. The areas of openness and trust have more than eight (8) behaviors, but they have been mathematically controlled to be equal with the other subscales.

In order to determine why one area or variable is high or low, it is necessary to view a report (see Appendix B) that gives scores for each of the behaviors that operationalize that culture or climate variable. All of the items that measure a given variable are grouped for each of the 11 subscales. To the left of each item under the heading "average response" is the average score on that item. Scores of 4.0 or better indicate areas where performance is good and faculty "agree" that the behavior is present. Scores below 4.0 indicate areas that can be improved. Keep in mind that some (those italicized) items are reverse scored, for example, item 40. If it is below 4.0, then faculty agree with the negative statement and believe that morale is low.

Suppose, on the other hand, the committee chose a different quantitative survey to measure school climate, like the Organizational Climate Description Questionnaire (OCDQ) and described by Hoy and Hoy (2006). This survey measures the behavior of the principal and teachers on six climate dimensions. The principal's style of interacting with others is measured as supportive, directive, and restrictive. The teachers' behavior is measured as collegial, intimate and disengaged. Based on the scores from the survey, the behavior is coded as open, engaged, disengaged, or closed. Scores can be graphed to quickly see strengths and areas needing improvement.

If a quantitative survey is chosen to collect data on the school's climate or culture, there are a number of things to consider. One consideration is whether culture or climate data are wanted or if data on both are wanted. Another consideration is the length of the survey. The OCQ is very short, with only seven responses, and takes faculty about five minutes to complete. The IIS has 96 behaviors and takes faculty about 30 minutes to complete. The OCQ is a measure of seven broad categories of behavior, and the IIS measures 96 very specific behaviors.

A major consideration should be how helpful the data are in developing the school improvement plan. For example, suppose there is a low score on the OCQ for the climate variable organizational clarity. How helpful is this score in developing the school improvement plan? On the other hand, if there is a low score on the IIS for the climate variable sense of mission, there are also scores on eight behaviors that make up this variable. By looking at the scores for each behavior that operationalize this variable, the committee would have some guidance in developing a plan to improve scores related to sense of mission. The above comparison is designed to provide the reader with some things to consider when a decision is made on selecting a survey instrument for the collection of climate and/or culture data. A number of surveys that collect data on a school's culture and climate are described by Stolp and Smith (1995).

If a qualitative survey such as the force field analysis were used to collect the data, the task of analysis becomes a little harder. For example, if there are 50 faculty members on the staff, there will be 50 sheets of paper to be analyzed for themes or repeatedly occurring behaviors. Often there will be a number of behaviors that say similar things, but the wording could be different. This requires some judgment to paraphrase what the central behavior might be. For example, there could be 20 "better if" comments about faculty meetings, but many of them say different but similar things. Analyzing all this data and writing the report for themes about the forces for and against a good school culture requires time and effort.

GETTING FEEDBACK FROM THE FACULTY ON HOW TO IMPROVE THE CLIMATE AND/OR CULTURE

The first step in getting feedback from the faculty on how to improve the climate and/or culture is to share the results of the quantitative or qualitative assessment. Based on the report, the strengths and areas needing improvement are identified. If the IIS were used to collect the data, it is recommended that one culture variable and one climate variable be identified as the two areas needing improvement. The reason for this recommendation is that the variables are all highly related. Bulach (2002) concluded, "The correlations for the 11 culture and climate factors with each other tend to be very high with expectations and assessment/time on task being the highest with a correlation of +.939" (p. 2). Since the variables are highly correlated, any change in one of the variables will result in positive changes in the other. According to Reeves (2004), it is important that the school improvement plan be successful. A focus on one culture and climate variable is more likely to accomplish success. The shotgun approach of developing a plan targeting all 11 variables is less likely to be successful because of lack of focus.

In selecting the culture and climate variables, group openness is almost always the culture variable with the lowest score and the lowest relationship with the other culture and climate variables. According to Bulach and Williams (2002), "The low correlations for openness are probably a result of the two dimensions measured by this factor. Openness has a telling and a listening dimension. Faculty can be very open on one dimension and closed on the other and vice versa. For this reason, correlations tend to be low for openness with the other factors" (p. 2). Past experience in working with more than 100 schools indicates that this culture variable should not be the variable targeted for improvement, even if it is the lowest score.

This recommendation is based on two reasons: (a) because of the low correlation with the other variables, a change in this variable will have less of an impact on the other variables; and (b) because openness is the most difficult to change. Improving levels of group openness requires time for faculty to communicate and interact. Finding time for faculty to do this is very difficult because of schedules and the way schools are organized.

The behaviors associated with group atmosphere or group cooperation are much easier to change, and they have a strong relationship with the other variables. The school identified in Appendix A chose group atmosphere as the culture variable most needing improvement. They chose discipline as the climate variable most needing improvement. Based on their plan, they made significant improvements on these two variables and on all other culture and climate variables. The overall culture and climate score went from 31.09 to 34.32 ($p < .01$). All other scores with the exception of group openness improved to 32.00 or higher. A score of 32.00 is an agree response that those behaviors occur. Scores approaching 40.0 are a strongly agree response.

With that as background, how can the entire faculty be involved in coming up with the school improvement plan? For the sake of explaining this process, the culture variable group atmosphere and the climate variable discipline are used. Following delivery of the report to the faculty, some form of the following instructions from the school improvement committee (SIC) can be given:

> We want your assistance in coming up with ideas on how to improve the behaviors associated with group atmosphere and discipline. We will give the chair of your group a packet of 3×5 or 4×6 index cards (size of the card is not important). Please review the eight behaviors associated with each of these variables, and pick two behaviors for each variable where you would like to see improvement. Write the behavior you would like to see changed on the card. Next write down one thing about that behavior that needs to improve or change to make you more positive about that behavior next year when the IIS is again administered.
>
> Follow the same process for each card that you turn in to your group leader. You can use as many cards as you wish, but you are being asked to turn in at least four and identify two behaviors and two things you would like to see changed for each of the two variables targeted for improvement. Your leader will sort the cards for areas or behaviors where there is agreement regarding changes and write a report stating these changes. The report and the cards turned in by your group will be given to the SIC.

When the report and cards are turned in to the committee, the cards can quickly be sorted into piles of common behaviors for each variable. Based on the reports and the data from the cards, the committee can identify which of the eight behaviors in group atmosphere and discipline will be targeted by the school improvement plan (SIP). Based on the reports and the data on the cards, there will also be a number of faculty suggestions regarding what needs to be changed to get a more positive score on that behavior. For example, the two group atmosphere behaviors targeted by the faculty of High Performing Elementary School (see Appendix B) were the following:

1. The administration shows favoritism to some constituents.
2. Faculty and staff morale at this school is low.

Based on the data from the reports and cards, it was discovered that the principal was sending the same people to conferences and workshops. The committee recommended that each group be allowed to decide who would represent them at conferences. While there were a number of other behaviors targeted by the SIP, this practice seemed to be causing the most problems. Scores on these two behaviors improved from 2.81 and 2.89 to 4.55 and 4.79, respectively.

When the cards and reports for discipline were analyzed, the following two behaviors were identified as those most in need of improvement:

1. The procedure the administration has in place for office referrals and discipline is effective.
2. The degree of communication with teachers about an office referral is appropriate.

Based on suggestions of what needed to be changed for the faculty to be more positive about these two behaviors: A written communication system was developed for office referrals. Teachers were sometimes sending students to the office without a written note, and the principal was sometimes sending students back to the classroom without a written explanation of what had been done.

There was a lack of consistency with the way discipline was administered. Further investigation, as the SIP was implemented, revealed that teachers were sending students to the office for being disrespectful, disruptive, rude, uncooperative, and so forth. These were judgments and not specific behaviors that made it difficult for the principal to correct misbehavior. The principal required that teachers write the specific behavior that caused the teacher to make that judgment about the student. The attitude adjustment or punishment that the principal used was much more specific and successful in correcting student behavior. Scores on these two behaviors improved from 2.76 and 2.95 to 4.24 and 4.32, respectively.

A similar process can be used if the qualitative survey is used to collect data about the climate and culture. For example, if in reviewing the forces for and against for themes, it was discovered that there were a number of faculty statements against faculty meetings. The 3 × 5 card system could be used as described previously. Each faculty member would write one thing on each card that, if changed, would make them more positive about faculty meetings.

The force field analysis process, as mentioned by the authors in chapter 2, can also be used for parents and students to get their input about the forces for and against a high-performing school. Once parents and students identify the forces against, the same 3 × 5 card method can be used to get ideas on what needs to be changed. The concept of the caring learning environment, as illustrated by the paradigm in chapter 2, has to be reinforced for improved student achievement.

The use of the 3 × 5 card method, shows that control is shifted and the leader is listening and cares about their feelings and thoughts. This leads to greater levels of openness, trust, risk-taking, and ultimately higher student learning and achievement. This entire process is enhanced if servant leadership is being practiced by the administration and faculty. An explanation of how students can become servant leaders can be found in chapter 5.

In addition to analyzing the data and using faculty feedback to develop the SIP, there are additional suggestions. Bulach and Berry (2001) investigated the impact of teacher experience on their perception of a school's culture and climate. Their research involved 1,163 teachers from 25 schools in Georgia. They found that teachers with two to five years of experience have the poorest perception of a school's climate, followed by teachers with six to ten years of experience. They found that teachers who were in their first year were also more positive than teachers with two to ten years of experience. Additionally, teachers with the most experience had the most positive perceptions of their school's culture and climate.

One other finding was that female faculty members have a much more positive view of a school's culture and climate than male members. Consequently, the development of a SIP should give some thought to how faculty members with two to ten years of experience are being supported after their first year and further whether there are any differences that might exist between how male and female faculty members are treated. Finally, the SIP must be implemented, and periodic meetings of the SIP committee should occur to see how the plan is working and if changes need to be made. The force field analysis process described earlier could be used to get feedback on the SIP.

COMPARING THE PRE-SIP DATA WITH POST-SIP DATA

The final step of Phase 1 is repeating the process for collecting the data that was used to develop the SIP and comparing it with the data after one year of implementation of the plan. An example of a pre- and post-comparison using the IIS can be found in Appendixes A and B. The use of the graph allows for easy detection of the success or lack of success of the SIP. The use of the report for each of the behaviors permits school officials to determine what behaviors caused a culture or climate variable to change. Hopefully, the one culture variable and the one climate variable that were part of the SIP have improved. The SIP for the next school year should again include one culture and one climate variable. The selection of the targeted variables should be based on input from the entire faculty. Once the variables are selected, the 3 × 5 card method should again be used to get faculty input to help develop the SIP for the next school year.

If the qualitative force field analysis is used to collect data, there are two ways to measure the success or lack of success of the SIP. The first comparison should be to look at the number of comments received about the targeted variable. If the targeted variable was faculty meeting, are there fewer comments in the better if or forces against section of the force field? Are there more comments about faculty meetings in the forces for section? For example, count the positive comments that faculty made in the pre-data (forces for), and compare that with the number of positive comments in the post-data. Since the size of the faculty can change from year to year, the data used for this comparison should be the number of positive comparisons for each faculty member. For example, if there are 50 faculty members and 150 pre-positive comments (3.0 per faculty member) about why they like working at the school and 200 post-positive comments (4.0 per faculty member), then the SIP has been successful.

The same process can be used to compare the pre-negative forces against with the post-negative forces. Hopefully, the number of times post-negative forces are mentioned per faculty member has decreased. The objective of the SIP should have been twofold: a) to increase the number of times forces for are mentioned and b) to decrease the number of times forces against are mentioned. This process takes qualitative data and allows the leader to look at it from a quantitative approach as well. It is important to look at the frequency of positive and negative comments per person. This is particularly important if comparisons are made between student or parent data as their numbers can change a great deal from year to year.

CONCLUSION

The process described by the authors in chapter 3 completes Phase 2 and continues the servant leadership and shifting of the control culture concept. The administration and faculty continue trust building by showing that they are willing to listen and that they care about the opinions of subordinates. The importance of teachers working together and the principal's role in focusing faculty attention on learning was supported by DuFour (2002). As stated by the authors in chapter 2, the mission of a high-performing school should be to focus on the continual improvement of instruction in a caring learning environment. The vision of how to accomplish this mission can be illustrated by the learning paradigm described in that chapter—that is, personal growth or learning starts with listening, and that leads to the belief that the leader cares. This creates an environment for servant leadership, openness, trust, risk-taking, and personal growth or learning.

APPENDIX A

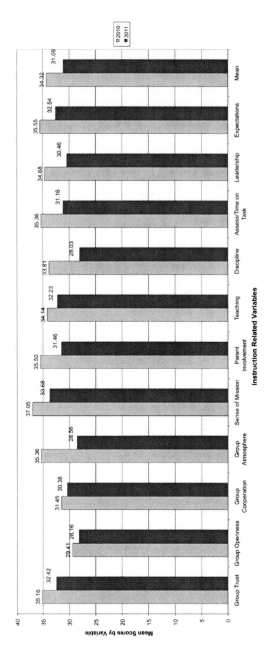

Figure 3.1

APPENDIX B

High-Performing Elementary School: A Measure of School Culture and Climate

The measure of school culture has four variables: (a) group openness, (b) group trust, (c) group cooperation, and (d) group atmosphere. The measure of school climate has seven variables: (a) sense of mission, (b) instructional leadership, (c) student discipline, (d) parent involvement, (e) assessment/time on task, (f) teaching practices, and (g) expectations. All items in italic are negative and must be reverse scored.

Definitions of each variable and the items that measure them are:

Group Trust: An interpersonal condition that exists when interpersonal relationships are characterized by an assured reliance or confident dependence on the character, ability, predictability, confidentiality, and truthfulness of others in the group.

Item	Mean Scores		
	2011	**2010**	
15	3.90	3.62	*Question others' intentions and/or motives.*
16	3.23	3.30	*Conceal your true feelings to what others do and/or say.*
17	4.23	4.03	Count on others for assistance.
18	4.59	4.05	Believe that others care about you.
19	4.45	3.76	Deal with them directly when there is a problem.
20	4.68	3.95	Expect that they will respond favorably in a situation where your welfare is at stake.
21	4.59	4.14	Rely on them to keep a confidence.
22	4.50	4.16	Believe they are honest.
23	4.59	4.49	Count on them to do what they say they are going to do.
24	4.68	4.43	Tell the truth when it needs to be told.
25	4.77	4.51	Respect the opinions of your colleagues.
26	4.68	4.38	Admit mistakes and/or problems when necessary.
27	4.41	4.19	Support their ideas, decisions, and actions.
28	4.23	3.73	Behave consistently regardless of the person, situation, or level of stress.

Group Openness: An interpersonal condition that exists between people when 1) facts, ideas, values, beliefs, and feelings are shared; and 2) the recipient of a transmission is willing to listen.

Item	Mean Scores		
	2011	**2010**	
5	3.32	3.49	Tell others what you think of the way they do things.
6	3.59	3.49	Tell others what you think of their ideas, values, and beliefs.
7	3.91	3.76	Express your feelings.
8	3.82	3.27	Ask others what they think about the way you do things.
9	3.68	3.00	Ask others what they think about your ideas, values, and beliefs.
10	4.05	3.62	Ask others about their feelings.
11	4.00	4.19	Accept others' comments and reactions.
12	3.23	3.43	Disagree with others if you don't agree with what is being said or done.
13	4.00	3.76	Share positive thoughts with others instead of keeping them to yourself.
14	3.18	3.16	Share constructive criticism with others instead of keeping it to yourself.

Group Cooperation: An interpersonal condition that exists between the various constituents (teachers, staff, students, parents, and community) in the school setting.

Item	Mean Scores		
	2011	**2010**	
48	4.18	3.70	Teachers are involved in the decision-making process.
49	4.23	3.76	A school leadership team or advisory council assists the administration with decisions.
50	1.95	3.81	A student leadership team or advisory council assists the administration with decisions.
51	3.91	3.86	A parent leadership team or advisory council assists the administration with decisions.
56	4.18	3.54	The administration keeps the constituents in the school setting adequately informed.
57	4.41	3.97	The constituents in the school setting are encouraged to communicate with the administration.
63	4.32	3.81	The degree of cooperation between the faculty and the administration is appropriate.
64	4.27	3.92	The degree of cooperation between the faculty and the staff is appropriate.

Group Atmosphere: A supportive interpersonal condition that exists between the constituents (teachers, staff, students, parents, and community) in the school setting.

Item	Mean Scores		
	2011	**2010**	
29	4.36	4.14	The feeling that people care about each other is present in the school.
30	4.82	4.31	The physical condition of the school facility is acceptable.
31	3.64	2.84	*People at this school complain a lot.*
40	4.79	2.89	*Faculty and staff morale at this school is low.*
41	4.64	4.27	Teachers are sensitive and responsive to the needs of students.
45	4.36	3.46	The administration is sensitive and responsive to the needs of teachers.
46	4.55	2.81	*The administration shows favoritism to some constituents.*
47	4.27	3.57	There is a feeling of togetherness/community at this school.

Sense of Mission: The degree to which the faculty agrees on a philosophy of education and is committed to the school's goals and objectives.

Item	Mean Scores		
	2011	**2010**	
32	4.68	4.62	The school's mission is posted for everyone to see.
33	4.50	3.81	A short phrase that captures the school's mission has been developed and placed in conspicuous places, e.g., on stationery, buses, etc.
34	4.50	4.22	The administration creates opportunities for the mission/vision to be shared with constituents.
35	4.77	4.62	The faculty was involved in creating the mission.
36	4.77	4.24	*A mission statement has been created, but it is not seen or shared.*
37	4.55	4.41	The faculty is in agreement as to the mission of the school.
38	4.77	4.11	*The mission statement is of little value for what happens at our school.*
39	4.50	3.65	If asked, the faculty are able to describe the school's mission statement.

Parent Involvement: The administration has created an environment that encourages parents to be involved.

Item Mean Scores
      2011 2010

Item	2011	2010	
42	4.50	3.76	Parents are recruited to serve as volunteers at the school.
43	4.27	3.97	The administration supports some form of media (newsletter, computer, etc.) to communicate with constituents on a regular basis.
44	4.41	3.86	The relationship that exists between parents and the teachers is a good one.
52	4.09	3.78	The relationship that exists between parents and the administration is a good one.
53	4.59	4.16	It is easy for parents to find out how their child(ren) is/are doing academically.
60	4.45	3.95	It is easy for parents to find out what their child(ren) must do for homework.
61	4.73	4.22	The administration has recruited business/community partners.
62	4.45	3.76	Volunteers who participate at the school are recognized for their efforts.

Teaching: The degree to which teachers use appropriate instructional strategies to promote student achievement.

Item Mean Scores
      2011 2010

Item	2011	2010	
54	4.59	4.32	Teachers vary their instructional strategies according to the needs of the students.
55	4.55	4.24	The behavior of the teachers communicates that they care about their students.
58	4.45	3.86	Homework assignments are appropriate for the student and subject.
59	4.59	3.86	Teachers explain the objective(s) of the activity or lesson for the day.
71	2.68	3.67	*Teachers at this school are unable to control students in their classroom.*
72	4.36	4.03	Teachers motivate the students to want to learn.
77	4.27	4.03	Teachers review previous work before introducing new material.
78	4.64	4.19	Teachers help students to feel good about themselves.

Discipline: The degree to which the administration and teachers are able to control the behavior of the students.

| Item | \multicolumn{2}{c}{Mean Scores} | |
	2011	2010	
65	4.55	4.35	The atmosphere in the classroom is conducive to learning.
66	4.24	2.76	The procedure the administration has in place for office referrals and discipline is effective.
67	4.32	2.95	The degree of communication with teachers about an office referral is appropriate.
73	4.50	4.05	*Students' safety is a problem at this school.*
74	4.09	3.27	The administration supports teachers in matters related to student discipline.
82	4.18	3.65	The responsibility for student behavior is shared by staff/faculty members.
83	4.18	3.65	Communication with parents about student misbehavior is appropriate.
84	3.95	3.35	The administrative plan for dealing with student absences and tardies is appropriate.

Assessment/Time on Task: What the teachers and administration do to monitor student achievement and time on task.

| Item | Mean Scores | | |
	2011	2010	
68	4.55	3.76	Student achievement data are monitored by the administration.
69	4.50	3.68	Student achievement data are used to provide feedback to teachers.
70	4.36	3.62	Student achievement data are used to evaluate the effectiveness of a program or change in the curriculum.
75	4.55	4.11	Teachers' grading practices are based on a variety of activities that monitor student learning.
76	4.41	4.11	Classroom instruction starts and ends on time.
88	4.41	3.95	The administration does their best to minimize time lost due to pull out programs and/or extracurricular activities.
89	4.36	4.14	The administration does their best to minimize time lost due to classroom interruptions.
90	4.23	3.81	Teachers' classroom management practices are effective in keeping students on task.

Instructional Leadership: What the administration does to improve student achievement.

Item	\multicolumn{2}{c}{Mean Scores}	
	2011	**2010**	
79	4.27	3.57	The amount and type of feedback the administration gives teachers is appropriate.
80	4.55	4.00	The administration makes sure that teachers have adequate materials and supplies.
81	4.27	3.78	*The principal spends too much time in the office.*
91	4.41	4.05	The administration uses staff development plans to promote student achievement.
92	4.55	4.30	The administration provides opportunities for teachers to grow professionally.
93	3.95	3.76	The administration empowers the faculty and staff.
97	4.27	3.59	The principal organizes and plans so that things run smoothly.
98	4.41	3.41	The administration knows what is happening in the classroom.

Expectations: Those teacher and administrator behaviors that tell students what is expected.

Item	\multicolumn{2}{c}{Mean Scores}	
	2011	**2010**	
85	4.32	3.89	Teachers make an effort to motivate those students who have low interest in schoolwork.
86	4.50	4.32	Teachers believe that every student can learn and improve.
87	4.45	4.22	The administration has high expectations for teacher performance.
94	4.59	4.05	The teachers have high expectations for student performance.
95	4.41	4.14	Students are given opportunities to show that they are responsible.
96	4.36	4.05	Teachers stress continuity of learning and make connections between subject matter taught.
99	4.36	3.84	*Teachers place too much emphasis on rote learning.*
100	4.55	4.03	*The use of workbooks, worksheets, and other fill-in-the-blank-type materials is excessive.*

REFERENCES

Berger, R. (2003). *An ethic of excellence: Building a culture of craftsmanship with students*. Portsmouth, NH: Heineman.

Bulach, C. R. (2002). An instrument that measures a school's culture and climate. A presentation at the American Educational Research Association Conference, New Orleans, Louisiana, April, 2002.

Bulach, C. R., & Berry, J., (2001). The impact of demographic factors on school culture and climate. *Resources in Education* (ED 462 744).

Bulach, C. R., & Williams, R. (2002). The impact of setting and size on a school's culture and climate. *Resources in Education* (ED 467 672).

Cunningham, W. G., & Gresso, D. W. (1993). *Cultural leadership: The culture of excellence in education*. Needham Heights, MA: Allyn & Bacon.

Danielson, C. (2002). *Enhancing student achievement: A framework for school improvement*. Alexandria, VA: Association for Supervision and Curriculum Development.

DuFour, R. (2002). The learning-centered principal. *Educational Leadership*, 59(8), 12–15.

Fullan, M. G. (2009). *The challenge of change : Start school improvement now!* Thousand Oaks, CA: Corwin Press.

Hoy, A. W. & Hoy, W. K. (2006). *Instructional leadership: A research-based guide to learning in schools*. Boston, MA: Allyn and Bacon.

King, D. (2002). The changing shape of leadership. *Educational Leadership*, 59(8), 61–64.

Lunenburg, F. C., & Ornstein, A. C. (2012). *Educational administration*. Belmont, CA: Wadsworth Publishing Company (6th edition).

Marzano, R. J. (2003). *What works in schools: Translating research into action*. Alexandria, VA: Association for Supervision and Curriculum Development.

Reeves, D. B. (2004). *Accountability for learning: How teachers and school leaders can take charge*. Alexandria, VA : Association for Supervision and Curriculum Development.

Senge, P. M. (1990). The leader's new work: Building learning organizations. *Sloan Management Review*, 32(1), 7–23.

Stolp, S., & Smith S. C. (1995). *Transforming school culture: Stories, symbols, values, and the leader's role*. Eugene, OR: Eric Clearinghouse on Educational Management.

Chapter 4

Power and Authority: Nine Techniques for Motivating Faculty and Students

Phase Three (When to use the freeing forms of power and when to use the controlling forms?)

In chapter 1 (Phase 1), the importance of shifting control to faculty and students was explained. This was a very important part of creating the high performing school culture. In chapter 2 (Phase Two), the authors described the importance of servant leadership and how to identify and reshape the culture of a school. In chapter 3, suggestions are given on how to implement a plan for continuing to improve the culture and climate of a school. In chapter 4, the authors describe Phase 3 of the process for creating a high-performing school. The focus is on how school administrators, teachers, and faculty use power and authority to either give control or take control. All principals and teachers have a form of power called position power where they take control, and this gives them the authority to reward and/or punish faculty and students.

The way leaders use power to influence and motivate subordinates* determines the kind of control culture that is created. According to McDowelle and Buckner (2002), "All the theories about how leaders use power, influence, and motivation are flawed. The most valuable thing we know about leadership is that no single theory or approach will work in all situations" (p. 18). The key leadership words here are influence, motivation, and power, and no single approach will work in all situations. Rather, there are nine different ways or forms of power that can be used by a leader to motivate and influence others (Bulach, 1999).

In this chapter, the authors describe these nine distinctly different forms of power. The use and misuse of these forms of power are also described. Five are "freeing" forms of power. They give subordinates control without giving

---

*When the words "leaders" and "subordinates" are used, the words "administrators and/or faculty" and "students" can be substituted.

65

up control. They are intrinsic motivators, and they give leaders a systematic framework for adapting their leadership style to create a culture where subordinates are motivated to grow professionally. When these five forms of power are used, servant leadership is the style being used.

The other four forms of power are "controlling" forms. They are extrinsic motivators and restrict and control the actions of subordinates. When these four forms of power are used to meet the needs of the people and the organization, servant leadership is still the form of leadership being used. When they are used to meet the individual needs of the leader, (self-serving) servant leadership is not in place.

A THEORY OF LEADERSHIP AND MOTIVATION

Many successful school leaders are embracing the concepts of total quality management, teamwork, and shared decision making as a way of empowering subordinates. Burns (1994) discussed this concept of empowerment and claimed that it is a "buzzword" and that often subordinates are not really empowered. He maintains that leaders should create conditions where subordinates are able to empower themselves. In other words, an organizational culture has to be created where "empowerment can come to life" (p. 48).

The problem of how to give control without giving up control and create conditions to empower subordinates is further exacerbated if the leader's style does not lend itself to shared decision making. Many leaders have a directive style with a high need to control. Leaders with this style tend to resort to position, reward, and coercion power to control subordinates.

Dilenschneider (1994) stated that when authority and power are practiced by directive, they will not continue to work. Further, he wrote that if power is the ability to get things done, it must be done through others. A key word here is the word "through" as opposed to the word "with". Directive leaders tend to get their work accomplished "with" the help of subordinates rather than "through" their help.

Debruyn (1986) maintained that the only way to keep power is to share it. He believes that many leaders abuse power, and in the end they lose it. The key is to share power and allow subordinates to have some control over the decision-making process. According to Bennis (1958), power is defined as control. He who controls has power, and if subordinates are given some control of the decision-making process, they are being empowered. Not only are they being empowered, but as Haskin (1995) stated, involving subordinates in the decision causes them to take more responsibility for the outcome of the decisions.

This increased responsibility tends to boost the power of the leader (Lammers, 1967). One such organizational plan for implementing a shared decision-making process and empowering subordinates was described by Bulach (1978). His plan requires that all teachers, administrators, and support staff serve on one of 25 committees that meet monthly to make decisions about curriculum and other district initiatives.

Some subordinates, however, are immature and do not want to be involved in the decision-making process. Hersey and Blanchard's (2007) theory of situational leadership requires that a leader consider the maturity or immaturity level of subordinates in selecting a style of leadership. A person with low motivation and little expertise is classified by Hersey and colleagues as immature, and the appropriate leadership style is to be directive.

According to Hersey and Blanchard when subordinates become more motivated and experienced, a leader's style should be modified. For example, if subordinates are very immature, a directive style of leadership will work, and a collaborative or nondirective style will not. This is not to say that one should not try to empower them, only that the leader has to be more creative in moving them from a low maturity level to a higher level. Modifying a leader's style requires the use of differing forms of power. For example, position, reward, and coercion power, or the controlling forms of power, are normally used with immature subordinates, while the freeing forms of power may be all that are necessary with mature subordinates. These forms of power are used when the leadership style is collaborative or nondirective.

PURPOSE OF THIS CHAPTER

In this chapter, the authors aim to describe a style of leadership where the five freeing and four controlling forms of power can be used to motivate and empower subordinates depending on their maturity level. Leaders must be able to influence and motivate subordinates both intrinsically and extrinsically. The nine forms of power are described and categorized according to the extent that they are intrinsic or extrinsic motivators and foster dependence or independence. The use and misuse of these forms of power are also described.

As mentioned earlier, the key words used to describe leadership are power, influence, and motivation. These words and other key terms described in this leadership theory are defined as follows:

- power: the ability to influence, control, and empower others.
- influence: the ability to motivate others.

- motivation: a process that causes others to sustain or change a behavior as a result of an extrinsic or intrinsic source.
- leadership: something that occurs when the leader motivates others (through use of the nine forms of power) to sustain or change a behavior.
- dependence: the subordinate is controlled (disempowered) by the leader, and the motivation is extrinsic.
- independence: the subordinate is in control (empowered), and the motivation is intrinsic.
- empowerment: giving subordinates control of the decision-making process and allowing them to be independent of the leader.
- disempowerment: the subordinates do not have control of the decision-making process, and they are dependent on the leader.

Variations of the above definitions occur with the two different types of these nine forms of power. The two different types are: (a) those freeing forms that involve subordinates in the decision-making process; and (b) those controlling forms that tell subordinates what to do. The five freeing forms of power are intrinsic motivators, foster independence of the leader, and empower subordinates. This occurs because subordinates are in control of the decision-making process. They are allowed to respond to a given situation and decide what to do. These forms of power are called freeing forms of power because subordinates are free to decide what will be done. They are given control of the situation, but the leader has not given up control.

The four controlling forms of power are extrinsic motivators, foster dependence on the leader, and disempower subordinates. This occurs because subordinates are not in control of the decision-making process. These forms of power are called controlling forms of power because subordinates are told what to do (controlled) by the leader.

WHY ARE CARING BEHAVIORS AND CONTROL IMPORTANT FOR AN EFFECTIVE SCHOOL CULTURE?

We believe that there are two fundamental needs that determine human behavior, whether in a classroom, school, home, or community. Those two needs are the need to have some control over your life and existence and the need to feel/believe that others care about you. We are presenting a theory of life or human behavior here with which you may agree or disagree. In order to give some background on how we came up with this theory, we cite the work of Nietzsche (1910). He examined other philosophies on why people behave the way they do. One such philosophy was that people behave the way they do because they want to be happy. Another philosophy at that time was that people behave the way they do because they want to be alive. They want to live and that's what motivates them to behave the way they do.

Nietzsche looked at these philosophies and disagreed. He theorized that there was a more essential need and that was the "will to power." He theorized that the need for power was more essential than life or happiness. We tend to agree with Nietzsche's theory, but we look at power as control. With power you gain control and what is life, if you do not have control. The feeling is one of hopelessness and not a good one! Just look at human history and the wars that have been fought to gain control. We can also look at U.S. diplomacy and how we use our military and money to control what happens in other countries. This feeling of being controlled by the United States, in many instances, is resented and not appreciated. In chapter 1, we presented the high performing school culture and how to give control to students without giving up control. However, we tend to disagree that human behavior is only about control.

There is another fundamental need and that is the knowledge and feeling that others care about you. This topic was covered in depth in chapter 2 where five sets of behaviors that create a caring learning environment were presented. They are:

- anxiety-reducing behaviors
- listening behaviors
- rewarding behaviors
- recognition behaviors
- friendship behaviors

According to the theory presented in chapter 2, if a student believes no one cares, learning will not take place. Instead unhappiness, poor attendance, dropouts, and even suicide are likely results. In this regard the U.S. diplomacy is on target. More than any other nation in the world we care about what happens in the rest of the world, but how about our classrooms and schools? The organization called the Eunice Kennedy Shriver National Center for Community of Caring at communityofcaring.org is a good resource on the importance of caring behaviors in a school. If you agree that being cared for and having control are important for an effective school culture, then you will find the nine forms of power great tools for helping to create a culture where these two essential needs can be met.

THE NINE FORMS OF POWER

French and Raven's (1959) original typology of power included five forms of power: (a) expertise, (b) referent, (c) position, (d) reward, and (e) coercion. These forms of power are included in the nine forms of power described in this chapter. We have added information, connection, moral, and ego power to the original typology of power. Information power was first described by Raven and Kruglanski (1975). Connection power was described by Hersey and Goldsmith (1980). Moral power was described by Sergiovanni and Starratt (2006). Ego power is Bulach's contribution and is described later in this chapter.

FREEING FORMS OF POWER

There are five freeing forms of power: (a) information, (b) expertise, (c) personality, (d) ego, and (e) moral power. We call these freeing forms of power because they give control without giving up control. We use the word empowerment with the freeing forms because giving control to others is a form of empowerment.

The first form of power is information power. Dilenschneider (1994) maintained that knowledge is power. Knowledge is information, and it is used daily by the news media to influence their audience. According to Toffler (1990), knowledge or information is the most versatile form of power. He wrote that it requires the least amount of energy and provides "the biggest bang for the buck" (p. 16).

Information can be used by a leader to involve subordinates in the decision-making process and empower them. For example, if the leader wants subordinates to change the way they are doing something, the leader can explain the benefits of the change. Handouts, videos, or other information extolling the advantages of the change can also be made available. Subordinates, after analyzing the information, need to make a decision. If subordinates decide to change, they are empowered, and the motivation for the change is intrinsic. The decision is made independent of the leader.

Expertise is the second form of power. The use of expertise also allows subordinates to choose a course of action. A leader who has expertise can demonstrate how to perform a task. Subordinates who watch the demonstration decide whether they are able to perform that task. Dilenschneider (1994) maintained that competence or expertise is the root of power and that leaders without competence cannot maintain power.

While he is correct, in today's complicated world, a leader cannot be an expert in all things. Consequently, leaders sometimes have to use the expertise of others to motivate subordinates to change. For example, if a new technique will benefit an organization, the leader can send key subordinates to another organization where that technique is being successfully utilized. The subordinates could observe the new process and decide whether it is beneficial and if it will work in their organization. Subordinates who are exposed to this form of power frequently choose to imitate or adapt what they have observed. It is their choice—the motivation is intrinsic; they are independent of the person with the expertise; and they have been empowered.

It is easy to confuse information power with expertise power because a person who is an expert in their field usually has lots of information about that profession. Information power, as used here, however, always refers to some type of language: for example, written, verbal, video, and so forth. A teacher might implement integrated thematic instruction after reading a report on how it improves student achievement. Expertise power, however, occurs when someone physically demonstrates something or sees it happening. If the same teacher observed a teacher who was an expert on this type of instruction, that would be expertise power.

Information and expertise power are often combined. For example, when an expert shares information, it is more powerful and carries more weight than if the information came from a less reliable source. It is for this reason that experts tend to be used by advertisers when products are being promoted—for example, basketball shoes and Michael Jordan.

A leader who has personality, or referent power, is described by Hersey and Blanchard (2007) as a person who is generally liked and admired by others because of personality and that is what allows them to motivate and influence others. When this form of power is used by a leader, it usually comes in the form of a request (verbal) or signal (nonverbal). The subordinate hears the request or sees the signal and changes behavior to comply with the leader's wishes. The change in behavior is done willingly and is intrinsically motivated, and the subordinate remains independent of the leader. The subordinate makes a conscious decision to grant the leader's wishes.

A form of power not previously mentioned in the literature is ego power. This form of power is used when the leader goes to a subordinate and says something like, "You did a beautiful job organizing that last project! Would you be willing to take responsibility for this one?" Another example might be, "If anybody here can handle this, I am confident you can!" When ego power is used, the subordinate's self-esteem needs are filled, and the subordinate is willing to take on and is open to the new experience. The subordinate voluntarily chooses to follow the leader's wishes. The subordinate remains independent of the leader, the motivation is intrinsic, and the subordinate has been empowered.

Ego power can be used in its negative form as well. For example, the leader might say, "I don't know, this might be too difficult for you. What do you think?" Another example might be, "The people over at Plant B or School A are able to produce a better product than us. Are they better than we are?" The use of the negative ego stroke can be perceived by the subordinate as a challenge.

A real live example of this negative ego stroke is Muhammed Ali, who is quoted in a Bottom Line Personal pamphlet as saying that his teacher told him when he was 12 years old that he would never amount to anything. After winning the Golden Glove for boxing at the 1960 Rome Olympics, the first thing he did was go to that teacher and show her his medal and tell her that "he was the greatest." This is a powerful leadership technique because subordinates who rise to this challenge tend to be very motivated. The subordinate sets out to prove to the leader, as did Mohammed Ali with his teacher, that they do have the ability that has been challenged. Again, the subordinate remains independent of the leader, the motivation is intrinsic, and the subordinate has been empowered.

Moral power is the fifth and final freeing form of power that empowers subordinates. It allows them to remain independent and is an intrinsic motivator. Sergiovanni and Starratt (2006) described moral power (authority) as the obligations and duties derived from widely-shared values, ideas, and ideals.

Leaders who use this form of power have vision and mission statements that convey expectations and a handbook that contains rules and regulations. They also use the "expectations diagnosis" in chapter 2 to arrive at a consensus regarding a set of expectations that describe what subordinates value and believe should occur in that organization. Everyone, if they abide by these expectations, is under the influence of moral power because it is the right thing to do. This form of power, once in place, requires very little effort from the leader other than to remind subordinates who are not living up to expectations of the right thing to do.

A servant leader who uses these freeing forms of power is involving subordinates in the decision-making process and creating conditions for them to grow. A quote from J.Martin Kohe at this website *http://thinkexist.com/ quotation/the_greatest_power_that_a_person_possesses_is_the/264215. html* is the following: "The greatest power that a person possesses is the power to choose." When administrators and teachers use these forms of power, they are allowing choice and developing leadership capacity in subordinates. Lambert (2003) described the importance of developing leadership capacity for lasting school improvement. She described a high-performing school as an institution where "the principal shares power skillfully with teachers, parents, community members, and students" (p. 9). When administrators and teachers share power, they are giving control to others without giving up control, and that is a key component of the high performing school culture.

CONTROLLING FORMS OF POWER

The next four forms of power disempower subordinates because subordinates are controlled by the leader, subordinates are dependent on the leader, and the motivation is extrinsic. They are (a) connection, (b) position, (c) reward, and (d) coercion power.

The first controlling form of power is connection power. Hersey and Goldsmith (1980) described this form of power as the perceived association a leader has with other influential people. If a subordinate perceives that a leader is well-connected with superiors higher in the hierarchy, their power is enhanced. The subordinate knows that the leader has a greater ability to reward or punish than someone who is not so well connected. When this form of power is combined with position power, it gives the leader greater status and increases the likelihood that compliance/control will occur.

This form of power is different from all of the other forms of power. The other forms are gained because of something the leader does. This form is acquired through the eyes of the beholder. If they perceive that the leader has power, then the leader has power whether he or she has it or not. The motivation is extrinsic because the subordinate makes a decision to follow the leader based on the subordinate's perception that the leader's connections could result in some future benefit. The subordinate does what the leader asks or tells them to because of a belief that the leader can follow through with a future reward or punishment as a result of compliance or noncompliance.

Position power refers to the authority and responsibility that have been assigned to a person holding an office. Position power is employed when the leader tells or orders a subordinate to do something. If a leader is liked, trusted, and respected by those superiors to whom the leader reports, position power is great. If the reverse is true, position power is weaker. When a leader uses his or her position to make a subordinate do something, the subordinate's motivation for doing things is extrinsic and the subordinate remains dependent on the leader.

Leaders who acquire position power also receive reward, coercion, and often connection power. Subordinates can either do what the leader directs them to do or suffer the consequences (coercion). Many leaders who rely on position power use rewards to motivate subordinates to do what they are told. When rewards fail to get the desired results, coercion or punishment is often used. If necessary, this type of leader may use their connection power to increase their ability to reward and/or punish.

One interesting phenomenon is that position power depends a great deal on connection power. If subordinates perceive that the leader does not have connection power, then the leader's position power is weakened. For example, if subordinates know that the leader's contract has not been renewed, the leader's ability to use position power to tell subordinates what to do is greatly weakened.

In the final analysis, leaders who use the controlling forms of power rely on rewards and coercion as the major sources of motivation. This is not to say that these forms of power should not be used. For example, if a leader has very immature subordinates, the controlling forms of power are most effective. With position power there are obligations and responsibilities to meet organizational needs. When subordinates fail to meet organizational needs, position, reward, and coercion power must be used. Lambert (2003) stated that leaders must deal with resistant teachers who refuse to participate in productive ways. The same holds true for teachers with their students. The controlling forms of power must be used with immature resistant subordinates. The servant leader must serve both the needs of the organization and the needs of those subordinates who are more mature and motivated.

The error that many leaders make is using these controlling forms of power immediately without allowing subordinates to respond to one or more of the five freeing forms of power. One of the goals of servant leadership is creating situations where subordinates can make decisions independent of the leader. This empowers them and fulfills some of their needs, while at the same time meeting the needs of the organization. Use of the five freeing forms of power also requires less effort than use of the four controlling forms of power. The ability to use the controlling forms of power can also be exhausted, where the freeing forms are almost inexhaustible. The primary objective of school administrators and teachers is to give subordinates control within a highly controlled environment without giving up control.

OVERUSE OR MISUSE OF THE NINE FORMS OF POWER

Overuse or Misuse of Information Power

Withholding information as a form of control over subordinates is not a good leadership technique. When information is withheld, subordinates are dependent on the leader for information and are kept in a subservient state.

Subordinates in this type of organization tend to dislike the leader, and morale is low. Since the leader has the information, the subordinate remains dependent on the leader. Fiore (1999) found that leaders in organizations with negative cultures communicate with subordinates only when there are problems—that is, they withhold communication—while leaders in organizations with positive cultures were excellent communicators.

A second misuse is too much information. The more information a leader shares with subordinates, the greater the chance that some information will be misinterpreted or that subordinates will experience an information overload. Determining the amount and kind of information to share with subordinates is a key leadership decision.

Overuse or Misuse of Expertise Power

Demonstrating expertise too often or when it is not necessary can be viewed as being self-centered or "showing off." A leader must communicate altruistic tendencies (concern for others over concern for self) if trust is to develop. Subordinates have to believe that the leader cares about their welfare. Appearing self-centered or as a "show-off" is contrary to servant leadership. The secret to expertise power is for leaders to allow "others" to demonstrate their expertise and use theirs only when it is necessary.

Overuse or Misuse of Personality Power

Most leaders will readily admit that they frequently use this form of power to influence subordinates. However, leaders need to be cautioned because this form of power can be easily overused. For example, a leader can go to key personnel with requests too often and cause subordinates to grumble and make comments like "Here he or she comes again. I wonder what they want this time?"

Overuse or Misuse of Ego Power

Knowing who to stroke and when to stroke an ego is a judgment call. Negatively or positively stroking egos too often can be viewed as manipulative. If the positive ego stroke is used too often, subordinates might perceive that they are being used. Negatively stroking an ego can also garner the opposite result. For example, if the leader tells subordinates that a task might be too hard for them, they might agree that it is too hard. The negative ego stroke is one of the most powerful leadership techniques a leader can use. If done properly, the subordinate will overcome all obstacles to meet the challenge; however, it must be done with subordinates who have strong egos.

Overuse or Misuse of Moral Power

Attempting to use moral power is a mistake when there is not an agreement on the expectations, values, and ideals that are to govern behavior. If agreement does not exist, the leader is imposing his/her set of values on the subordinates. This is contrary to the servant leadership concept. One of the first things a leader should do as the new head of an organization is foster a common understanding and agreement of the expectations that are going to be enforced and the values that are going to be rewarded. The process of arriving at this common understanding of values and beliefs is described in chapter 2 in the "expectations diagnosis."

Overuse or Misuse of Position Power

The overuse or misuse of position power can quickly extinguish its influence. Subordinates will rebel against the leader or undermine the leader's authority to the extent that organizational needs are no longer being met. The leader's superior(s) may transfer or fire a leader who cannot meet needs. The underuse of position power can lead to similar consequences. If a leader has position power, he or she must use it when subordinates and superiors expect it to be used, or they will lose it. Once subordinates determine that a leader is reluctant to use position power, they will begin challenging decisions, thereby weakening the leader's position power, until finally the leader loses his or her position in the organization.

Overuse or Misuse of Reward Power

Failure to reward people when they are deserving can cause severe morale problems. Leaders who have favorite subordinates who receive greater rewards than those who are less favored are misusing reward power. Lunenburg and Ornstein (2012) described Porter and Lawler's (1968) "equity/expectancy theory" of motivation. The essence of the theory is that when some employees receive greater outcomes (rewards) for the same input, there is a lack of equity. Those who receive less reward for the same input will perceive it as a lack of equity or fairness and be less motivated. Another mistake is to overuse reward power to the point that the reward loses meaning. Overuse of this power can create a "what's in it for me" mentality, where subordinates will not work unless they know they will be rewarded.

Regarding rewards as a source of motivation, Sergiovanni and Starratt (2006) stated that there are three ways to motivate subordinates:

1. the "what gets rewarded gets done" approach

2. the "what is rewarding gets done" approach
3. the "what is good gets done" approach

The primary objective of reward power should be to move subordinates from what gets rewarded to what is rewarding and good. What gets rewarded is an extrinsic motivator, and what is rewarding and good are intrinsic motivators; however, this form of power is the one controlling form of power that can be used by a leader for all subordinates regardless of their level of maturity. Even mature subordinates enjoy rewards. Consequently, leaders should not think of this as a form of power to use only with immature subordinates. One objective of leadership is the judicious use of reward power along with the five freeing forms of power.

Overuse or Misuse of Coercion Power

Leaders who quickly resort to coercion as a way to induce subordinate compliance will soon lose their position for the same reasons as the misuse of position power. Bullying behavior is one other misuse of coercion power that often occurs. There are bullies in many organizations who coerce their colleagues. *The Atlanta Journal-Constitution* featured an article on bullying behavior that stated, "Bullying—one of the most insidious and fastest-growing forms of workplace violence—is on the rise worldwide" (Joyner, 1999, Section R-1, p. 1). Leaders must act to curb bullies who are coercing their colleagues. Bullying behavior has become particularly prevalent in the school setting. Leaders must become more cognizant of bullying behavior.

Overuse or Misuse of Connection Power

Misuse of connection power is often associated with the use of threats regarding what to do if a subordinate does not comply with a request or demand. For example, "I am going to tell the boss if you don't get to work!" Use of this power in this way implies that a leader is not going to use his or her own power. Failure to use position power when necessary always weakens the leader. According to Cohen (2002), when position power is not used, the result is to make the other person more important, and this can lead to greater problems.

Another misuse of connection power is the leader who tries to create the illusion of this form of power by name dropping. Leaders who drop names are trying to create the illusion that they are connected. This practice tends to decrease the leader's power because subordinates often see through this ruse.

CONCLUSION

The five freeing forms of power—information, expertise, personality, ego, and moral power—can be used to motivate subordinates by empowering them. They also give control without giving up control. When used properly, the servant leader can use them to help move subordinates from one level of maturity to higher levels of maturity. When these forms of power are used, the subordinate decides the course of action. If they decide to follow their leader, the form of motivation is intrinsic because they see that course of action as a good thing to do. Further, they are allowed the independence of choice, and they are empowered in the process. As subordinates become more mature, the leadership style can become more collaborative and less directive.

The four controlling forms of power—connection, position, reward, and coercion power—should be used with immature subordinates, but only when the above five freeing forms of power do not work. These forms of power must be used by the servant leader if the freeing forms of power are not motivating subordinates and when subordinates are not meeting organizational needs. Keep in mind that the judicious use of reward power, while not a freeing form of power, nevertheless, is a good form of power. When these forms of power are used, subordinates must comply or face the displeasure/position power of the leader and forego the reward or receive a punishment/coercion. Subordinates have no choice, are in a dependent position, and are being controlled by the leader. Connection power enhances a leader's position power and increases his or her ability to reward or punish.

Who has the most power is an interesting question. A leader who has position power and connection power will be very powerful, only if they use the five freeing forms of power. All leaders have the ability to use all nine forms of power. Those leaders that use all nine will be very powerful. Those that use only the controlling forms and occasionally some of the freeing forms will be less powerful.

The goal of servant leadership should be to move away from the old forms of bureaucracy that rely on position, reward, and coercion power toward a high-performing culture that relies on information, expertise, personality, ego, and moral power. A bureaucracy fosters dependency and relies on extrinsic motivation, whereas a high-performing school empowers faculty and students and relies on intrinsic motivation. In a bureaucracy, leaders control subordinates to make sure they do things right (position power), as opposed to a high-performing culture where the focus is on doing the right thing (moral power).

The objective for leaders is to create an organizational culture where subordinates are actively involved in the decision-making process. In order for this to happen, the leader has to be less controlling and give control without giving up control. Remember, that the need for power and control is a fundamental cause of human behavior. The five freeing forms of power are leadership techniques that allow this to be accomplished. The word "freeing" is used because the subordinate is independent and "free" to make their own decision. They have the power and are in control. When subordinates do not do the right thing, the controlling forms of power must be used to make them comply. The word "controlling" is used because the subordinate is dependent and does not have "control" of the decision.

Knowing when and how to free subordinates and give them control (empower) and when to take control (disempower) is the *sine qua non* of effective leadership and being able to motivate subordinates. While this chapter describes the role of the servant leader with subordinates, the reader needs to keep in mind that the same principles apply to a teacher as the servant leader for students in a classroom. Whether as a teacher, principal, parent, or any other role, a servant leader gives control without giving it up, empowers others, helps others, shares leadership, creates independence, builds trust, and creates a caring learning environment where everyone is focused on how to improve things for others. We believe that there are two fundamental needs that determine human behavior, whether in a classroom, school or anywhere: They are the need to have control and the need to believe that someone cares about them.

REFERENCES

Bennis, W. G. (1958). Authority, power, and the ability to influence. *Human Relations*, 11(2), 143–155.

Bulach, C. R. (1978). An organizational plan for curriculum development. *Educational Leadership*, 35(4), 308–314.

Bulach, C. R. (1999, November). Motivating subordinates: Nine leadership techniques. A presentation at the Southern Regional Council of Education Administration, Charleston, North Carolina.

Bulach. C. R. (2001). A four-step process for identifying and reshaping a school's culture. *Principal Leadership*, 1(8), 48–51.

Burns, G. (1994). The trouble with empowerment. *Quality Digest*, 14(2), 47–49.

Cohen, A. H. (2002). *Why life sucks and what you can do about it.* San Diego, CA: Jodere Group.

Debruyn, R. L. (1986). The only way to keep power. *The Master Teacher*, 18(6), 1–2.

Dilenschneider, R. L. (1994). *On power.* New York: HarperCollins.

Fiore, D. J. (1999). The relationship between principal effectiveness and school culture in elementary schools. Unpublished doctoral dissertation, Indiana State University, Terre Haute, Indiana.

French, J. R. P., & Raven, B. (1959). The bases of social power. In D. Cartwright (Ed.), *Studies in social power* (pp. 150–167). Ann Arbor: University of Michigan, Institute for Social Research.

Haskin, K. (1995, April). A process of learning: The principal's role in participatory management. Paper presented at the annual meeting of the American Educational Research Association, San Francisco, California.

Hersey, P., & Blanchard, K. (2007). *Management of organizational behavior.* Englewood Cliffs, NJ: Prentice Hall.

Hersey P., & Goldsmith, M. (1980, April). The changing role of performance management. *Training and Development Journal,* 34(10), 18.

Joyner, T.(1999, August 29). Bullies on the rise. *Atlanta Journal-Constitution,* Section R-1, p. 1.

Lambert, L. (2003). *Leadership capacity for lasting school improvement.* Alexandria, VA: Association for Supervision and Curriculum Development.

Lammers, C. J. (1967). Power and participation in decision-making in formal organizations. *American Journal of Sociology,* 73(9), 201–216.

Lunenburg, F. C., & Ornstein, A. C. (2012). *Educational administration.* Belmont, CA: Wadsworth Publishing Company (6th edition).

McDowelle, J. O., & Buckner, K. (2002). *Leading with emotion: Reaching balance in educational decision-making.* Lanham, MD: Scarecrow Press.

Friedrich Nietzsche (1910). "The will to power. An attempted transvaluation of all values. Books one and two". In Oscar Levy. *The complete works of Friedrich Nietzsche.* 14. Edinburgh and London: T.N. Foulis. http://www.archive.org/details/completeworksrie033168mbp.(Revised third edition 1925, published by The Macmillan Company).

Porter, L. W., & Lawler, E. E. (1968). *Managerial attitudes and performance.* Homewood, IL: Irwin Press.

Raven, B. H., & Kruglanski, W. (1975). Conflict and power. In P. G. Swingle (Ed.), *The structure of conflict* (pp. 177–219). New York: Academic Press.

Sergiovanni, T., & Starratt, R. (2006*). Supervision: A redefinition* (8th ed.). New York: McGraw-Hill.

Toffler, A. (1990). *Powershift.* New York: Bantam Books.

Chapter 5

A Character Education Program That Is the Foundation of a High-Performing School

Phase Four

In chapter 1 (Phase I), we described the four types of school cultures and provided data on how the high performing school culture improves time on task, improves school culture and climate and eventually improves test scores. A process for identifying and reshaping the culture of a school is described in chapters 2 and 3 (Phase 2). In chapter 4, the use and misuse of the nine forms of power and their impact on a school's culture and climate are described (Phase 3).

According to Walsh (2004) and Berger (2003), the entire school community must be involved to create a high-performing school. Berger stated: "Though society debates the question of whether schools should teach values, the process of schooling itself imbues values—we have no choice about this. If we want citizens who value integrity, respect, responsibility, compassion, and hard work, we need to build school cultures that model those attributes." (p. 7) That is the purpose of the character education program we will describe in this chapter.

Thus far, a vision has been created for a high-performing school (chapters 1–4), and the vision has been implemented; however, a process for involving the parents and community has not been developed. While there are many ways to accomplish this involvement, one method is the implementation of a character education program. In this chapter we will describe a character education program, and why such a program is important for a high-performing school. We will also describe how "social contracting" can play a role in a character education program and a high performing school.

WHAT IS A CHARACTER EDUCATION PROGRAM?

A character education program is any effort to shape student, faculty, and community behavior related to selected character traits. According to Bulach (2002), a character trait is something that affects a person's relationship with others; however, Bulach also said that there is a self component for some character traits, for example, persistence or responsibility. Consequently, he defined a character trait as an intrinsic attitude or belief that determines a person's behavior in relation to "other people" and in relation to "self." Further, he stated that all character traits fall into one of two groups: those that determine how we behave with others and those that determine our self behavior. Such character traits as sportsmanship, generosity, kindness, respect for others, courtesy, and empathy have behaviors associated with them that are easily observable in relation to other people. Such character traits as persistence, responsibility, honesty, self-respect, and self-control have behaviors associated with them that relate more to self and are not easily observable. Consequently, there are two types of character traits: those that relate to self and those that relate to others.

Many schools in the United States have mandated character education programs, but according to Prestwich (2004), there is little agreement on how teachers and school officials should approach this task. Bulach (2003a) found school officials using a variety of different curriculums for their character education programs. Some schools have purchased canned curriculums, and others have developed their own. Some have set aside a certain time of the week to deliver the character education curriculum or have delivered it while a certain subject is being taught, and others have infused it throughout the day. Some schools focus on a character trait of the week and others a character trait of the month.

Bulach (2003a) recommended that schools align their curriculum so traits that relate to others are the focus in one semester and traits that relate to self are the focus the next semester. He stated that mixing the two does not allow for curriculum scope and sequence. For example, respect for others, courtesy, kindness, and compassion all have similar behaviors that relate to others. Conversely, persistence, responsibility, accountability, dependability, honesty, and self-respect have similar behaviors that relate to self. When grouped by type, teaching one reinforces the others.

WHY IS A CHARACTER EDUCATION PROGRAM IMPORTANT IN A HIGH-PERFORMING SCHOOL?

In 25 schools in Georgia, Bulach (2003b) found a correlation of $+.71$ ($p < .01$) between the culture and climate of a school and student behavior related to 16 sets of character traits. In 193 schools in West Virginia, he found a significant positive relationship $+.34$ ($p <.00$) between achievement and character scores. Since there is a significant statistical relationship between culture and climate, character behavior, and student achievement, it makes sense to include a character education program as an integral part of a high-performing school. This program, if it is to be successful, must involve the entire school community—faculty, students, parents, and all other citizens. Implementation of this program is Phase 4 of the plan for a high-performing school.

IMPLEMENTING A CHARACTER EDUCATION PROGRAM

Current character education programs focus on a character trait of the week or month and tend to be cognitive in orientation. This creates three problems: **First**, the focus tends to be on knowledge of the trait rather than the behaviors associated with the trait. This creates a situation where students may know more about a trait, but the behaviors associated with that trait have not changed. The student also receives mixed messages about a trait because faculty members have different interpretations of it.

The **second** problem is the level of commitment of the faculty. Some faculty members do not participate in the character education program. Additionally, after a number of years doing the same trait of the week, boredom with the process begins to take place. Bulach (2003b) found that a number of schools, particularly at the middle and high school levels, had lower scores in year four of the grant than in year one. In questioning faculty and students about this decline, they stated that it was the same thing every year, and a lot of teachers had stopped doing it.

The **third** problem is the character education curriculum. Most state mandates require school officials to implement a character education curriculum. Typically, the character education curriculum focuses on a different character trait for the week or month. This change in focus on the next character trait makes it difficult to involve parents and the community. Involving parents and the community is essential for an effective character education program. If the character education program is to be successful, it must address these three limitations of current character education programs.

If parents and the community are to be involved, a school and/or school district should focus on a character trait for the year or semester. School officials do not have to change their current character education program—as many are required to do by law—to teach all character traits each year; however, they can focus on one trait per semester or year along with their current program. A great trait to start such a program is "respect for others" or "courtesy."

Littky and Grabelle (2004) maintained that respect for others or courtesy must be present in order to build and cultivate a positive school culture. They stated, "We must have and demonstrate respect for others, for ourselves, and for the building itself. If kids are going to be respectful, they must feel respected." (p. 55) Correlations on the 16 sets of character traits in the four-year Georgia study ranged from a high of +.97 to a low of +.80. Consequently, if behaviors associated with "courtesy" are improved, a corresponding improvement in behaviors associated with all other character traits will also occur. A survey that measures these 16 sets of character traits has been developed. A report, graph, and cover letter generated by this survey can be found at this website: http://www.westga.edu/~cbulach/.

IDENTIFYING THE BEHAVIORS ASSOCIATED WITH A TRAIT

It is important to identify the behaviors associated with a trait. It may have one meaning for a student from the projects, one meaning for a minority student, one meaning for a cook, one meaning for a bus driver, one meaning for a parent, and another meaning for people at a school in North Dakota versus one in Florida. How can school officials identify the behaviors associated with a trait for their school? The process is surprisingly simple as follows (again there is no magic in three 3 × 5 cards—use more or less as appropriate for your setting):

1. The teacher should give each student three 3 × 5 index cards and tell them that the focus of the semester (or year) will be on "courtesy". They should ask them what they would want people at the school to do or say to them to show them "courtesy.". The teacher should then instruct them to write one behavior on each card. Tell them they can't write "yes sir," "no sir," or "thank you," as these will occur on most cards.

2. The teacher should collect all the cards and sort them into piles of common behaviors. He or she should paraphrase those where there is agreement that a behavior is indicative of "courtesy."

3. Faculty members should also be given 3 × 5 index cards with the same instructions.

4. At some event where a number of parents are present, they should be given cards with the same instructions.

5. Business partners should be given cards with the same instructions.

6. All returned cards should be given to a committee or coordinator who identifies 10–15 behaviors indicative of "courtesy" at that school.

7. A chart of these behaviors should be made for each classroom, hallway, the cafeteria, and so forth. This chart should also be sent home for parents to place on their refrigerator or elsewhere.
8. The same chart should be sent to all business partners. If this is a district initiative as opposed to a school initiative, the chamber of commerce can be asked to make a copy of the chart for their members.

When the chart goes up at the school, at home, and at community businesses, everyone is likely to recognize a behavior they have written. Since everyone has been part of the process and recognizes their contribution, they are more likely to buy in and support the character education program. The identified behaviors can now be made a part of the high-performing school disciplinary program. The desired behaviors associated with the selected trait can be reinforced when they are seen, and when those behaviors have not been demonstrated, they can be extinguished through the use of redirects. Below are some behaviors that were identified using this process:

• Students interrupt when others are talking.
• Students use curse words or "bad language."
• Students call each other names.
• Students say things, like, "Thank you," "Pardon me,"
• Students listen when someone talks to them.
• Students ignore others.
• Students talk back to teachers and other adults.

The concept of servant leadership is also reinforced through the focus on "courtesy." When everyone is focused on showing courtesy to others, a fundamental change occurs in the school setting. Normally students, and to some extent faculty, tend to come across as self-serving. In related research, Bulach, Fullbright, and Williams (2003) found that 50 percent of students had a negative response on the behavior "people care about each other at our school." A focus on "courtesy" should decrease self-serving behaviors and increase serving others and caring behaviors. Everyone, including students, becomes a servant leader.

The above process requires no curriculum or time set aside to implement. Everyone, including cafeteria workers, custodians, bus drivers, and secretaries, can be involved in the process of reinforcing desirable behavior and extinguishing undesirable behavior. Parents and the community are also encouraged to participate in the character education program. The old adage that it takes a community to raise a child is now more likely to occur. According to Berger (2003), the culture that is created in a school has to be shared by parents and the community. He also believes that this shared culture impacts student achievement. Focusing on one character trait for a year or semester allows this shared culture to develop.

This process encourages reinforcement when a behavior associated with the trait occurs and legitimizes an intervention when behavior is inappropriate. It also heightens parent and community awareness of the behaviors associated with a character trait. In many instances, parents and the community have never really considered what "courtesy" looks like in the home and community. Also, in many schools, character education occurs during a set time during the week or day, and it is not emphasized the entire day. The end result is an emphasis on improving behaviors associated with this trait during the entire six to seven hour school day, as well as the rest of the day in the home or community.

The character education curriculum focused on one trait each year or semester is essential to create a feeling of community in the school and each classroom. This feeling of community, according to Berger (2003) is essential for an effective school. Students feel safe in this type of school culture. They do not fear being bullied. They do not fear the risk of failure. They feel supported at the school and at home and in the community. Everyone is focused on behaviors associated with one character trait.

The process can be repeated each semester or year for additional character traits. The next character trait that is recommended for focus is "responsibility." This trait determines behaviors related to self, while the previous one determines behaviors toward others. Of all the traits, with a correlation of $+.41$ (p $<.01$), it has the highest correlation with student achievement. The next semester or year should be followed with a trait related to behavior toward others and followed by one related toward self.

A good trait to follow "courtesy" is "respect for others," or if bullying behavior is a problem, "compassion" might be selected. A good trait to follow "responsibility" is "self-respect." This reinforces the efforts of the Safe and Drug Free federal mandate and helps reduce alcohol and drug abuse as well as sexual promiscuity. It also addresses the major school problem of cursing. The Bulach (2003b) research, in both Georgia and West Virginia, found that using foul language always garners the most negative scores. While we have stated that you can focus on one trait each semester, we recommend focusing on one trait each year. That way everyone is focused and committed and each year the focus is on a different trait. The current problem of boredom with most character education programs can be eliminated.

THE ROLE OF SOCIAL CONTRACTING

Social contracting has been discussed and written about for centuries and goes back to Jean Jacques Rosseau (1800). More information on social contracting can be found on this website: http://www.fordham.edu/halsall/mod/Rousseau-soccon.html. On page one at that site, we find these words:

"At a point in the state of nature when the obstacles to human preservation have become greater than each individual with his own strength can cope with . . ., an adequate combination of forces must be the result of men coming together. Still, each man's power and freedom are his main means of self preservation. How is he to put them under the control of others without damaging himself . . . ?"

A well designed character education program is focused on how people come together or treat each other and how they treat themselves (self preservation). It is also true that there are many obstacles to having a high performing school culture. That is why it would be very helpful if each student had some form of social contract regarding how they were going to behave in that school setting. The same could be said for all faculty at the school, but we are only going to focus on a social contract for students. We want the students to come together and agree on a set of behaviors that will guide student behavior at that school.

Keeping in mind that "each man's power and freedom are his means of self preservation" we need to give students some control over the process of social contracting, i.e., we need to give control without giving up control. Consequently, we advise letting students choose, from a set of behaviors, the ones they wish to govern their behavior. How this set of behaviors is developed is left to the faculty of each school. The behaviors at a rural school in Indiana could be quite different from a school in Atlanta, Georgia. Some examples of behaviors a student could choose from are the following:

- To do my homework.
- To stop using cuss words.
- To help a student who is being pocked on or bullied.
- To show respect and courtesy to others.
- To treat others the way I want to be treated.
- To tell the truth.
- To avoid the use of tobacco, alcohol and drugs.
- To pay attention in class.
- To help others who are having a problem.
- To do what teachers ask them to do.

The lead sentence for these behaviors should be "I will do my best" and then have the student select from the list of behaviors generated by the faculty at that school. By having students select the behaviors they agree to do their best to follow, you give the student control without giving up control. Since the students choose the behaviors they agree to follow, they are more likely to try and adhere to the contract they sign. How many behaviors they choose from the ones identified by the faculty is up to each school's faculty. They could choose 7–10 or less. Each faculty should make the decision on how many behaviors will be in the contract. The important thing is to let students choose the behaviors. If they are forced to choose all of them, then you have not given control, and the conditions of social contracting will have been violated. Also having the lead be "I will do my best," also gives them more control because it gives an escape when they are unable to comply with that behavior.

When and where this contract is developed and signed is up to each school's administration and faculty. Certainly, it should be as each new student is enrolled and in front of his/her parents or guardian. Whether the parent or guardian also signs the contract is your choice? We think it would be a good decision to have the parent or guardian also sign whenever possible.

There is another reason for a social contract. If you recall, we wrote that students needed to have some control over what happens to them, and they also needed to feel that caring behaviors were present. We also wrote that various philosophers stated that people behaved the way they do because they wanted to be happy and be alive. We also believe that there is a fifth reason why people behave the way they do. People, or in this case students, who have a purpose will behave differently than students who do not have a purpose. Having students develop and sign a social contract gives them a purpose. Dr. Mehmet Oz and Rick Warren are both strong proponents of a purpose driven life. If students are alive, are happy, have control, are cared for, and have a purpose, the five needs for why people behave the way they do are being met. The end result will be a school culture and climate for the creation of a high performing school.

CONCLUSION

The overall impact of counting redirects, servant leadership, giving control without giving up control, the freeing forms of power versus controlling ones, the character education program and social contract create a learning environment for a high-performing school. To use an analogy, think of baking a cake. In chapters 1–4, like mixing ingredients for a cake, the authors discuss the elements that must come together to create the ideal environment for a positive culture and climate. In chapter 5, the character education program and social contract can be compared to icing the cake. This is the final touch that brings everything together for the entire school community.

The end result is a combination of processes that go together in a seamless fashion. Each can stand alone, yet each supports and reinforces the other. If the mission is to create a high-performing school where students, faculty, and all other constituents are successful, this is a recipe or vision for accomplishing that goal.

THREE HYPOTHESES

If teachers have more time to teach, and if the time students are on task increases, it is logical that test scores should increase. We do know that 30 graduate students implemented a "high-performing classroom" where there were fewer discipline problems, teachers had more time to teach and the percentage of time students were on task did increase. We also know that four schools in Indiana implemented it on a school wide basis and that student time on task increased about 76 percent (described in chapter 1).

We also know that there is a significant positive relationship between a school's culture, student achievement, and character behavior. Consequently, it is hypothesized that: 1) any school that implements this reform will find an improvement in student achievement; 2) there will be a greatly reduced dropout rate because students will enjoy attending this kind of school; and 3) bullying behavior will be reduced. Students will feel empowered instead of controlled. They will feel like someone cares about them. They will be motivated both intrinsically and extrinsically (described in chapter 4). They will have a sense of belonging. Finally, parents and community will feel an association with the school and will reinforce student behavior related to 16 sets of character traits (described in chapter 5).

REFERENCES

Berger, R. (2003). *An ethic of excellence: Building a culture of craftsmanship with students*. Portsmouth, NH: Heineman.

Bulach, C. R. (2002). Implementing a character education program and assessing its impact on student behavior. *The Clearinghouse*, 76(2), 79–83.

Bulach, C. R. (2003a, November 16). A four-year character education grant: What have we learned? Presentation at the International Civic Education Conference, New Orleans, Louisiana.

Bulach, C. R. (2003b). West Virginia character trait report. Research report detailing the results of the status of character education in all 55 school districts in West Virginia.

Bulach, C. R., Fullbright P. J., & Williams, R. (2003). Bullying behavior: What is the potential for violence at your school? *Journal of Instructional Psychology*, 30(2), 156–164.

Jean-Jacques Rousseau, (1800) *Contrat social ou Principes du droit politique* (Paris: Garnier Frères), pp. 240–332, passim. Translated by Henry A. Myers.

Littky, D., & Grabelle, S. (2004). *The big picture: Education is everybody's business*. Alexandria, VA: Association for Supervision and Curriculum Development.

Prestwich, D. L. (2004). Character education in America's schools. The School Community Journal, 14(1), 139–150.

Walsh, J. A. (2004). Leadership for high-performance learning. *The LINK: A Publication for Education Practitioners*, 22(2), 1–3, 12.

Part II

Enhancing a School's Culture and Climate

In part I, the authors describe a four-phase process for creating a climate and culture for a high-performing school. In part II, we detail strategies for enhancing that culture and climate.

Chapter 6

Seven Strategies for Enhancing a School's Culture and Climate

In this book, the authors detail a process for creating a school culture and climate for a high-performing school. It allows school officials to be selective in how they go about creating that culture. Consequently, the four-phase process allows school officials to implement any one or all four of the phases described in part I. While implementing all four phases is advisable, each phase will result in an improvement in a school's culture and climate.

Implementing the concept of servant leadership is crucial to improving a school's culture and climate. This concept is embedded in each of the four phases. Phase 1 will result in the most improvement in a school's culture. This phase describes the high-performing school. With these thoughts in mind, this chapter describes seven strategies that will enhance the culture in part I.

STRATEGY 1: VISIBILITY BEFORE, DURING, AND AFTER SCHOOL[1]

The first strategy concerns visibility and how the principal must maintain a presence before, during, and after school. As the school leader, students, staff, and parents feel better when the principal is seen in the school and at different functions. Principals are the key to school climate (Hanna, 1998). As safety becomes an even greater issue in schools, visibility of the principal becomes even more necessary. It is easy to get tethered to the computer and phone in the office, but it is essential for the principal to be present and visible to students, parents, and staff. It is important for assistant principals, security assistants, and teachers to patrol the halls and campus, but it is imperative that the principal be patrolling and visible. The culture and climate of a school can be enhanced by the simple act of being visible.

A study by Hsiehe and Shen (1998) reviewed the traits of school leaders—characteristics and duties as seen by superintendents, teachers, and principals. Their research shows that visibility is a key element. Two factors affect a principal's success in establishing his or her presence at a school:

1. Flexibilty: A principal must be flexible to accommodate the changing needs and expectations of the community. After the Columbine High School and 9/11 tragedies, students, parents, and staff need now more than ever to see the principal in the halls, in classrooms, in the cafeteria, and before and after school at the bus loop. It is also important for students to hear his or her voice over the intercom during announcements.

   Staff and students are quietly reassured when they see the principal throughout the school day. This unfortunately puts more pressure on principals to be up and out of their offices, but paperwork can be done and phone calls made before students arrive and after students go home. It is ever important to be visible when students are at school.

2. Personality, attitude, and behavior: According to Hsiehe and Shen (1998), the principal's personality, attitude, and behavior play an important role in his or her leadership style. The ability to adapt to meet the expectations of the people being served is very important. After-school activities are very time-consuming for principals. Parents want and expect the principal to attend their child's soccer game. Assigning assistants is common practice, but parents still want to see the principal supporting their child.

Parents and students give more positive comments concerning a principal's presence at activities and games than any academic innovation the school might implement. If there is any doubt about this, consider school districts that have considered eliminating or cutting back on athletics, band, or cheerleading and the public outcry it caused.

A few years ago there was an ESPN special on eliminating sports in Mobile, Alabama, due to financial reasons. People all over the county expressed their dismay and chided the district for not wanting to cut unnecessary academic programs first.

It is common practice to assign other administrators to cover after school events, but a principal misses out on tremendous public relations opportunity when he or she does not attend. Selling tickets, working in the concession stands, sitting with the parents, and wishing the team and coaches good luck are just a few ways principals can mingle. The key is visibility and interaction—time spent answering questions, stopping rumors, and creating positive PR. School newsletters are often used for this purpose, but they are less effective than one on one interaction. If everyone knows they will be able to see and talk to the principal after school, they will seek him or her out to discuss concerns, problems, issues, and so forth. This greatly reduces the number of phone calls principals receive and improves interpersonal communications.

Principals should go to as many of the sports, PTSA, and club meetings as possible. Even after school practices are important events. They are additional opportunities to interact with students and parents in a less formal atmosphere. Cell phones and walkie-talkies allow the principal to return phone calls from anywhere in the building or on school grounds. Many school districts are purchasing cell phones and minutes for their principals. If not, remember that cell phones and minutes, when conducting school business, are tax deductible.

Visibility is very important in gaining trust and acceptance—key components of a school's climate. Creating time to be visible in a busy and crowded schedule is not an easy task. Delegation of duties to other staff members is one solution to this problem. It is important to establish a routine that is agreeable to everyone. The following practices will help principals arrange their time to allow for more visibility in their school.

• Assign daily activities to assistants: Try to meet with assistants during the summer to reorganize duties for the upcoming school year. Assistants are often more willing to assume extra responsibilities if they do not have to attend evening programs/sports. With the extra daytime duties being tended to by assistants, the principal is available to attend more athletic and other events. This helps keep assistants from "burning out" and allows the principal to get out of the office more.

• Coordinate with the secretary: Once the secretary is aware of this strategy, meetings can be scheduled with parents and students in the office or at events later that evening. The secretary should have a walkie-talkie or cell phone so he or she can remain in communication. Phones and walkie-talkies are worth their weight in gold as they improve communication and reduce the amount of time people spend looking for each other throughout the school. Teachers, students, and even parents can be met somewhere on campus as opposed to in the school office.

The time a principal spends walking through the school to ensure visibility can be quite productive. In addition to providing staff and students with the security of his or her presence, this time can also be used to make certain the school is running smoothly. The following techniques will help the principal be more productive while patrolling the buildings and grounds of the school.

- Vary the route: By varying the routine as the halls are patrolled, students and staff members can be observed in the right or wrong places. This can also be accomplished with security cameras, but it is more effective to see and be seen. Don't forget to check bathrooms and parking lots and other places where students are likely to hide.
- Carry a notepad, recorder, iPhone, or some other recording device to note things that need to be addressed but may be forgotten if they are not recorded on the spot, for example, missing ceiling tiles, teachers not on hall duty, graffiti in the bathrooms, and so forth.
- Stand in the hall during every passing period: Spending so much time in the halls can be a burden, but it is a necessary trouble and part of being visible. It is a good opportunity to greet students, call them by name, and make them feel they belong at their school. It also gives you an opportunity to see how the students treat each other and can head off potential problems.

Remember that paperwork and communication can be accomplished when students aren't on campus. Being visible during the school day and any other time students are present definitely will improve a school's culture and climate.

STRATEGY 2: CREATE A DUTY-FREE SCHOOL[2]

Another way to enhance a school's culture and climate is to create a duty-free school. Teachers and staff have enough to do each day, teaching students, planning, grading papers, talking with parents, and so forth. If there are things that can be done to take a few tasks off the faculty's plate, it is greatly appreciated. Note what can be done to relieve them of some of their non-teaching duties and let them concentrate on teaching.

For example, many school officials require that teachers walk their students to and from lunch every day, even though teachers do not walk their students to other classes. If teachers walk their students to lunch and pick them up after lunch, a 30-minute lunch period is reduced to 20 minutes. Also, try to expand the eating areas and the time for lunch to 45 minutes. Students in the middle and higher grades should be able to find their class and don't need to be walked. Teachers who have a duty-free lunch of 45 minutes will be very appreciative of the extra time. This is just one example of something that can be done to help school climate. It is simple and does not cost anything, but it can make a world of difference for the teachers.

The movement for school reform has affected everyone, but it does not seem to have had a great impact on relieving teachers of their non-teaching duties. State and federal directives seem to continue to pile on additional work. Principals should make it a priority to redirect teachers' time from supervision and paperwork to creating more time for instruction.

An interesting development in shared decision making—important in school reform—is that many principals have to add another duty to their teachers, and that is committee work—Q teams, study groups, school leadership teams, and research teams that help lead and manage the school. Research has found that such extra duties can take as much time as other traditional non-teaching tasks (Richardson & Sistrunk, 1989). In light of this finding, it is even more important to reduce duties not related to teaching.

As most principals know, teachers can resent assigned supervisory roles, especially when they believe those roles should be the sole responsibility of administrators. Teachers often view classroom interruptions and managerial tasks as overwhelming handicaps in their attempts to perform the core instructional tasks for which they were hired. Time that teachers do not have to spend on non-teaching duties can be spent teaching and preparing for class.

The strategy of creating a duty-free school must be carefully thought out and planned. The principal can work with teachers and staff to develop some ideas and possibilities. After carefully evaluating each possibility, a determination should be made of how many of the non-teaching duties can be reassigned, eliminated, or compensated for.

Changes that are not successful can be modified or dropped at any time. Even if conditions do not improve, teachers will appreciate your efforts in addressing their concerns. Remember that a key concept of part I of this book is servant leadership. Time spent on reducing non-teaching duties reinforces this concept.

Teachers must redefine their responsibilities to include a variety of non-teaching tasks. They must determine how much time to devote to non-teaching work and how much to spend on their core instructional tasks. They must develop ways to buffer their instructional role or face the prospect of experiencing a reduced commitment to their work.

School officials need to supervise students at least four times a day: before school, after school, during passing times (teachers are normally by their doors), and at lunch. Suggestions that might be useful to the principal and teachers are as follows:

- Give comp time to teachers for supervisory duty and other non-teaching activities.
- Have school administrators make a commitment to being on duty during critical supervisory times.
- Combine homeroom with first or second period to eliminate at least one passing period. Fewer students will be in the halls, and there will be one less class to supervise.
- Purchase walkie-talkies or cell phones for administrators and secretaries. They are extremely effective for campus coverage and will reduce the number of staff members required by enhancing communication capabilities. Keep in mind that walkie-talkies can be assigned to multiple staff members. If possible, do not overlook custodians. They are a crucial part of the school's culture and climate, and they often see things that administrators do not. They can provide additional eyes and ears.
- Invest in a security system that includes cameras. These are wonderful observation tools. Someone, such as a secretary or volunteer, should be assigned to monitor the security screen and call for assistance as needed.
- Purchase a golf cart or several carts if the campus is large. This is a great investment that allows school officials to cover a lot of territory quickly.
- Assign hall lockers near students' first period classes to reduce hall traffic.
- Close off specific areas of the campus to students before and after school and at lunch time.
- Position teams as close to each other as possible in middle schools, and in high schools, group classes by grade instead of by department to keep students in more easily monitored areas.
- Use parent volunteers to supervise, monitor, and chaperone when possible.
- Reduce the number of lunch periods to make monitoring less tedious. This means serving more students at each lunch and requires more lunchroom supervisors; however, the extra personnel are required for a shorter time period.
- Limit the number of faculty and department meetings to specific days and times that the faculty agrees upon.
- Use existing aides or hire others to supervise at lunch and other periods.
- Check with the central office about hiring a full-time substitute. On days when a teacher is not absent, the substitute teacher can be used creatively. The substitute can take over a mentor teacher's classroom so he or she can observe a first-year teacher who needs help.
- Allow teachers with first period planning to sign up for after-school coverage. Then allow them to come in late before their first class.
- Ask teachers with last period planning to sign up for before-school supervision, and then allow them to go home after their last teaching assignment.

- Reassign one period during lunch for cafeteria supervision, or have staff members interested in administration volunteer before and after school.
- Limit the number of parent conferences to only certain times and days of the week. Try to encourage parents to use e-mail or phone calls for conferences.

The administrative team must be diligent with their duty-related responsibilities. The extent to which the principal and the assistants are tied up in the office is the extent to which failure is predictable. Not only does a visible administrative team reassure the staff, their presence reminds the students who is in charge.

According to Potter (one of the authors), who was a practicing principal for years, the benefits to teachers are obvious. He stated the following:

As a principal, I was able to eliminate many duties at the schools where I worked. While I have not undertaken a formal survey to evaluate the effects of this policy, informal evidence and consistently positive responses proved that this was a strong climate booster. The extra time allowed teachers to perform many tasks that they would ordinarily do on their own time. My experience with eliminating teacher supervisory duty never compromised student safety or security. As in virtually every aspect of school life, success ends up being a combination of the administrator's supervisory diligence and everyone working together toward a common goal.

STRATEGY 3: MORE EFFECTIVE MEETINGS[3]

Teachers often dread meetings, and it is difficult to find a perfect time to meet. Principals need to think about their meetings and be conscious of the time that it requires of teachers. Poorly planned staff meetings can backfire, causing staff members to disregard important information. There are ways to efficiently and effectively share information with staff members.

A common practice for school officials is to require after-school meetings on a predetermined day. Generally they are "stand and deliver" assemblies presided over by the principal with his or her assistants seated nearby to lend credibility to what was being said and to give dirty looks to stragglers.

Over the years, a number of different practices have emerged for ensuring that faculty members receive important information. The following are some examples of those practices:

- One administrator checks the sign-in sheet against the faculty roster to determine who missed the faculty meetings.

- A secretary takes the minutes from faculty meetings to put into teachers' mailboxes so they wouldn't forget all the important information the principal had gone over.
- Tape recorders and video cameras are used to catch the essence of the content of the meeting.

This is not to say that faculty meetings aren't important. They can and should be; however, they should also be interesting so the faculty actually wants to attend and looks forward to them.

An interesting phenomenon about faculty meetings is that teachers often mirror the same poor behavior displayed by their students. Some will sit as far back in the room as possible, and if there aren't enough chairs back there already, they will move them. And some will talk, grade papers, read the newspaper, and generally not pay the least bit of attention to what the speaker is saying.

The need to share important information with staff members will always exist, but times have changed, and the usual ways of relaying information are no longer effective—if they ever were. When disseminating information, take a few minutes to disregard your current ideas of how information should be shared and adopt some more effective strategies.

Old Strategies

There are several examples of traditional means of disseminating information. Administrators can stand and deliver presentations, reading informational items to faculty members. They can also use daily written bulletins placed in teachers' mailboxes at the end of the day. The information is often old, and teachers are too tired to read and respond to any items. Bulletins are often found in the nearest trash can. A calendar or information sheet can be posted on the bulletin board; however, teachers are often too busy to stop and read the new information, or the information is so old that teachers have grown accustomed to passing by without notice. Morning and afternoon announcements can be made over the PA system, but these can be a terrible waste of teaching time. And meeting minutes can be recorded on audiotapes or videotapes by the school secretary, but they are quickly forgotten and gather dust.

New Strategies

Information that used to be shared during meetings can often be disseminated by some form of technology, such as a power point presentation, chat rooms, or e-mail. E-mail messages must be relevant, timely, and to the point. Staff members can read the messages when time permits, respond if necessary, and save when needed. Of course, all faculty must have computers and check their e-mail on a regular basis. Most staff members will become comfortable with computers and e-mail when they discover that doing so will eliminate many after-school meetings.

Move toward a practice of having a paperless environment so all communication is carried out through some form of technology instead of on a piece of paper. Power point presentations can be attached to an e-mail and viewed at leisure. Chat rooms can be set up so teachers can talk to each other and with the administration. There are ways to monitor electronic communications so school officials can ensure that all faculty are involved.

School officials need to make sure that every certified employee and most non-certified workers have their own computers and e-mail addresses. It is important that faculty have access to a technical support person. That person needs to train computer-challenged staff, fix small computer problems, and update information as needed.

Each school should have a website that tells about the school. This is a public relations tool that communicates what the school represents to the community and new parents. Many parents, when looking for a new home, surf the Internet and read school websites. These are the kind of parents you want in your school. They are involved, motivated, and tend to have kids who have high test scores.

Through use of technology, valuable faculty time spent in meetings can be reduced. Further, when there's an emergency, such as bad weather or a stranger in the building, an announcement can be made over the PA system that faculty should check their e-mail inboxes. This gets necessary information to staff members quickly without alarming students.

Common planning periods is another practical strategy that can be initiated for communication purposes, that is, one common planning time for all staff members before students arrive. If the school day starts at 8:55 a.m. for students, teachers and staff members can be required to report for work earlier. During that time, grade, subject, team, and faculty meetings can be held.

This is also a great time for parent–teacher conferences, which allow staff members to meet while they are still alert and does not intrude on their personal time after school. This also allows all the teachers who interact with the student to take part in the conference. In a one-on-one conference, parents can sometimes become belligerent in supporting their child. In a team conference with a parent, this is less likely to occur.

The usefulness of staff meetings shouldn't be determined by a meeting's time or format as much as the purpose of and need for the meeting. Administrators must plan staff meetings carefully. Informational meetings can be waived in favor of e-mail messages.

Staff members' valuable time should not be wasted by calling an all-staff meeting to distribute information that can be read or that only pertains to half of the teachers. This causes them to tune out office communications. Then, like the little boy who cried wolf, when something really important surfaces, they won't be listening, won't show up, or will be late. Staff members should be treated as professionals, and their planning time should be safeguarded.

Use meetings for relevant staff development training given by administrators, fellow teachers, or central office personnel. Remember that if the meeting is important enough to require staff members to attend, administrators need to be there as well. Show support for the program. Do not get a "sage on the stage," that is, someone who will discuss in 30 minutes or less the merits of a new educational philosophy to try at your school. Involve staff members in planning to ensure that the program is relevant to their work. The following questions can be used to gauge the importance of a meeting:

- Why do we need to meet?
- How is the meeting going to help students learn? Don't call a meeting just because it is the third Wednesday of the month.
- How does the meeting relate to the goals of the school? This process is very helpful to your school's climate, and it continues to reinforce the concept of servant leadership.

STRATEGY 4: HOSTING A SUCCESSFUL OPEN HOUSE[4]

An open house for parents is now required in many districts and states, usually in the early fall. The question is how to showcase the event so it becomes a positive public relations tool that improves the school's culture and climate. Often principals do what they have always done and do not attempt to improve the event each year. There is only one chance for a good impression at an open house as this is the only time that many parents will visit the school.

The tone and climate for the school year, as perceived by parents, is frequently set on that night. The format should change somewhat every year, based on what worked best the previous year. This is a good time to use the force field analysis technique presented in chapter 2. For example, faculty (one color) and parents (another color) could be given a sheet of paper on which the following instructions are found (complete these two sentences as many times as you wish):

I liked attending the open house because . . . (forces for)
Half way down on the sheet write this sentence:
I would have liked attending the open house better if . . . (forces against)

The use of different colors for parents and faculty allows for quick identification of responses. Based on the responses, it is easy to identify what went well and what needs improvement for the next open house.

Through use of this technique we have heard from parents who were really impressed with what they saw and heard during open houses. We have also received complaints as follows:

- I could not find the rooms.
- The building and grounds were dirty.
- The faculty was unprepared and/or not helpful.
- The open house was not well organized.

Let us give you a few examples of how we have used the data. On one occasion, we received 53 parent comments that the building was dirty. In showing them to the custodian, it was a wake-up call because he lived in the community and valued their opinions more than those of the administration and faculty. The cleanliness of the building immediately improved. Some other examples were, Mr. X could not explain his grading policy, Mrs. Y was not prepared, and Mr. M had a wonderful presentation. It is amazing the response when the administration meets with a teacher and presents the data—10 sheets of paper with a force "for" or "against."

One way to use this data is to hold a meeting with Mr. X and give him the ten sheets that say he could not explain his grading policy. Say nothing other than, "What do you think?" The urge to say, "This has to be corrected!" (ball is in your court) might be strong, but "What do you think?" (ball is put in Mr. X's court) is more appropriate. Mr. X can respond positively and agree, saying, "I was unable to explain it." In this case, the administration should respond with, "Okay, when do you want to meet so you can explain it?"

Of course many teachers will deny that they failed to explain it and come up with excuses why parents wrote that as a force "against" a good open house. If that is the case, the administration should employ a technique called the "broken record." After each excuse or denial, the administration should calmly state, "There are 10 parents who wrote that you could not explain your grading policy." Keep repeating (broken record) until Mr. X agrees to remedy the problem.

The leadership objective here is to get Mr. X to assume responsibility for his own ability or lack thereof. It is servant leadership at its best. The urge to control and make faculty adhere to the leadership of the administration has been kept in check. Instead data has been used, and based on the data, the faculty member has been given the opportunity to improve on his deficiency. Instead of using position power to get Mr. X to change, information and moral power presented in chapter 4 were used to correct a problem that has affected the school's culture and climate.

Getting feedback through use of the force field analysis technique is extremely important. It once again reinforces the concept of servant leadership. It demonstrates to everyone that you care about their opinion and are willing to take steps to meet their needs. The more the administration utilizes this technique, the greater the likelihood that faculty will also use the technique to get feedback from students and each other about their teaching, a field trip, a presentation, their discipline, their rules, and the list goes on. Remember that the concept of servant leadership must permeate the school's climate and culture.

Preparing for a successful open house begins with an assessment of the school's culture and climate far in advance (described in chapter 2). While a healthy school climate and culture are the underlying components of a successful open house, it is a great opportunity for enhancement as well. Just as we can observe whether someone is physically unfit or feel when a car is not running properly, parents can sense when things are not right at their child's school by what they see and hear when they visit.

There are a number of steps involved in planning a successful open house. Some things to consider are:

- Who will plan the event? Will a steering committee or the principal head the effort? Clearly define the roles and responsibilities and set up a communication and reporting system.
- What is a good date for the event? Check the school and district calendar and make sure no other events are scheduled in the feeder schools that would force parents to choose between events. Don't forget to consider other community activities or popular public events, such as the World Series or Monday Night Football. Stay away from Wednesday evenings as this is a church night in many communities.
- When is the right time to announce the open house? Send a notice home with students a few weeks in advance. Announce the open house in the media and by e-mail, if possible. Display information about the event on your message board about two weeks beforehand. To increase attendance, some schools have competitions among classrooms with prizes for the most parents in attendance.

There should be at least two news releases about the open house, one covering the same content as the notice to parents and the other a simple reminder to "mark your calendars for the upcoming open house and find out more about your school." The notice should include:

- what, when, time, and where
- how parents can get their child's schedule
- what parents should do if they want to privately discuss their child's performance
- what to expect at the open house (visiting classrooms, general assemblies, or both)
- where they should park
- where they should go when they get to the school
- whether they should bring their child with them

An open house should be no longer than an hour and a half to two hours. Plan to accommodate all three groups of people—parents, students, and staff.

Focus on Parents

The most effective open house begins with a formal informational meeting where principals share their philosophy and expectations regarding students' achievement and behavior. This is also an opportunity to alert parents to future events, testing, promotion requirements, and materials that will be sent home. If the force field analysis will be done, this is the time to pass out the paper with the two sentences asking them to give you feedback on the open house. Ask them to put their feedback in a box as they leave the building. Have a student waiting at the door with the box and extra forms in case parents have misplaced theirs.

This meeting should not last longer than 15 to 30 minutes. Parents are more interested in meeting their child's teachers than listening to administrators talk about the school. After the meeting, parents disperse and follow their child's class schedule. It is best to forego having food at the meeting. It slows down the start of the session and will make parents and students linger afterward so that they are late getting to classes.

Enlist Students

Students are a valuable resource for a successful open house. They can direct parking to smooth parents' arrival, and they can act as guides and greeters to lead parents to meeting places and classrooms. The students' behavior and demeanor is a strong indicator of the school climate, so take time to work with them prior to the event.

Prepare Faculty and Staff

Faculty and staff members are crucial in having a successful open house, and principals must prepare them well. The careful organizing will be for naught if teachers do a poor job in the classroom. Hold a faculty meeting early in the planning process to address concerns and expectations. Assign master teachers to mentor new teachers on conducting their mini-classes for parents.

Require teachers to file plans of how they will make use of the time parents are in their classrooms. Plans should focus on course objectives, not just instructional activities. Remind teachers that the open house is full of teachable moments and ask them to identify what they want parents to learn about their subject and classrooms. Assure teachers that the administration will be visible in the hallways and classrooms.

All staff members should be briefed on their duties, but the custodial staff is particularly important. The building should be spotless, floors should shine, and all trash should be removed. To accomplish this, it may be necessary to rearrange schedules so all custodial staff are available between the time classes are finished and when the open house begins. Remember this might be the only time some parents are ever in the school.

Bringing in additional custodial staff from other buildings is also an option if an agreement with another local administrator can be brokered. Make sure that someone checks the sound system, air conditioning, lights, and other electronic equipment that will be needed.

Other Considerations

There are some additional questions to address prior to staging an open house:

- How will parents learn about the media center?
- Will the PTSA and the parent volunteers have a sign-up table?
- Will there be student entertainment?
- Will the superintendent and school board members be invited?
- Will information be available to parents about tutoring, college, and careers?

A successful open house will accomplish your goals if it is planned, organized, and executed well and has a thorough follow-up. Also remember that open houses come in all shapes and sizes and can be held more than once a year. They can be scheduled at the beginning, middle, and at the end of the school year, after report cards to better prepare for the next semester, to meet staff, or just to get parents in the building so they feel more comfortable about having their child attend the school.

STRATEGY 5: MAINTAINING A VOLUNTEER AND MENTORING PROGRAM[5]

The accountability standards mandated by state and federal legislators are becoming increasingly difficult to meet. Using volunteers and mentors are one strategy that can go a long way toward helping meet accountability standards. There is a common belief that parental involvement and strong schools are inseparable and that one cannot exist without the other. Research also indicates a strong link between student achievement and parental involvement. What better way to get parents and the community involved than to get them volunteering at the school.

If community and parental involvement in the school are to be successful, there are a number of factors to consider. If their assistance is to benefit students and staff, the process has to be carefully structured. Often in public secondary schools, getting parents and the community involved is difficult. It can also be challenging to find volunteers willing to do the tasks that are really needed. Staff members may need one thing while the volunteers want to do another. All volunteers should be carefully screened before they are allowed to work in the school and with students. With the Jessica Lunsford law, it is important to have them cleared by the school and district.

Set Yourself Up for Success in a Volunteer Program

The principal must be the leader in the volunteer initiative. To have an effective program, a thoughtful and well-executed process must take place. Attention to the following elements will ensure a successful program:

- Identify and establish the needs of the school. Work with faculty, staff, students, and parent groups to determine what parental and community support are needed. Decide how volunteers can be most useful.
- Select a volunteer leader. If the volunteer program is to be a success, it must be done right. Make sure the selected volunteer faculty member takes this assignment seriously and gives it the time and effort needed. The program may be important enough to hire a full-time person to lead and manage the program. If money is not available, the best coordinator may be a volunteer rather than a faculty member. Sometimes this person can better deal with a problem volunteer than a faculty member, because he or she is a member of the community and knows the volunteer on a personal basis.
- Establish a selection process. It is imperative that volunteers be carefully selected and screened. Today, most districts do their own screening and processing. Know who they are and what they will be doing. Try advertising

for volunteers with local media outlets to get the word out. Obviously, parent groups like the PTSA, parents, and school business partners are great for recruiting. Local groups like the rotary, the chamber of commerce, retirement homes, grandparents, alumni, and college students can be great sources.

- Be specific about what is needed, the time commitment required, and who to contact for further information. Devise an application to gather important information from willing participants. Make every effort to talk and work with these volunteers prior to "letting them loose" in the building.
- Match needs with interests. Know the skills, interests, and limitations of the volunteers. Time, experience, and level of commitment are factors to be considered when trying to match a person to a job.
- Develop a volunteer training program. Reduce or eliminate the uncertainty of the volunteers by making sure they understand their responsibilities. Conduct orientations and be as thorough as possible. A volunteer handbook should be developed that lists school policies, phone numbers, names of administrators, the school calendar, and other useful information that will help the volunteers feel welcome.
- Monitor volunteers' time spent in the building. Develop a process for volunteers to check in and check out so there is a record of how much time each is spending in the building. Volunteers who spend the most time should be given special recognition to show appreciation for their services.
- Monitor and evaluate the activities. It is very important to monitor and evaluate volunteer activities to ensure that the program is benefiting faculty and students. If a program is not beneficial, then decide whether to discontinue the activity, modify it, or put a different volunteer in charge. Again, the force field analysis works well for this kind of evaluation. The volunteer program is good because . . . and would better if . . .
- Celebrate success. Be sure to thank your volunteers. They have done something to help the school and the students. They must be thanked in a sincere manner—verbally, in writing, and when possible, at a luncheon or banquet.

Building positive school, parent, and community volunteer relationships will improve school climate and make the school a better place. Some possible volunteer activities are:

- tutoring and remedial help
- mentoring
- heading academic booster clubs
- acting as volunteer coaches
- parent and teacher organizations

- arranging open house activities and meetings
- raising money for school projects
- acting as band, music, cheerleading, and athletic boosters
- working in the offices
- helping in the media center and with book fairs
- assisting in the classrooms
- helping with field trips
- acting as guest speakers in classes (many senior citizens with a wealth of knowledge and skills love to come to classes and share)
- acting as career day volunteers
- conducting workshops for staff (finance, retirement planning, computers)
- staging demonstrations in vocational and career classes
- taking part in adopt-a-student
- spending time on local school advisory councils
- participating in ad hoc groups
- acting as chaperones at dances and field trips
- selling tickets or working in the concession stands at games
- spending time on landscaping committees
- acting as medical people working with staff and coaches

Be creative. There are hundreds of useful and valuable ways to use volunteers. Everyone who wants to be involved and qualifies with your school can do something to benefit your students.

STRATEGY 6: DEVELOP A MENTORING PROGRAM FOR BEGINNING TEACHERS[6]

Mentoring is "a relationship in which a more experienced person facilitates the broad development of a less-experienced person on a regular basis and over an extended period of time" (Lankford, 1996, p.1). In its simplest form, a veteran teacher volunteers or is assigned to guide a novice teacher for a certain amount of time to help smooth the transition. How new teachers are mentored will likely determine how successful they become and how long they stay in the profession. Having a good mentoring program means a positive climate for new teachers and established teachers alike as many experienced teachers will work with the new ones. Work with central office in this endeavor, and the impact on faculty will be positive.

Research indicates that beginning teachers need to know and master a number of important ideas and concepts to be effective (Darling-Hammond, 1998). Beginning teachers should:

- Have a thorough knowledge of their content area.
- Know how a subject connects across areas of the curriculum and how these ideas can be successfully integrated with other subjects to ensure that what the student is learning is useful in everyday life.
- Understand that students are in different "spurts" of their cognitive, social, physical, and emotional growth.
- Learn how to motivate all students—those who are at risk, unmotivated, or have special needs.
- Learn how to care for all students, treating them with dignity and respect.
- Know the different learning styles, teaching methods, and strategies.
- Evaluate students' knowledge and assess students' approaches to learning.
- Know the latest in curriculum resources and technology.
- Use successful classroom management techniques.
- Have the ability to reflect on, critique, and improve their teaching.
- Know the academic standards and the curriculum of the school, district, and state.
- Understand that their major role is to serve the needs of students, i.e., servant leadership.
- Understand the various policies of the school, district, and state.

These items can be reinforced through a mentor relationship. The keen eye and sensitive ear of a mentor can provide a beginning teacher with necessary and critical support. If done correctly, mentoring is a valuable tool in helping beginning teachers improve in their profession, stay focused, and get acclimated.

If the school district does not have a formal mentoring program and one is needed, remember that it must be tailored to fit individual school needs. Mentoring programs can take many forms and serve several purposes. They can help a new teacher become better acquainted with the job of teaching, they can help them learn the "ropes," and they can help them accomplish more in the classroom.

It is best to allow the veteran teacher to select the new teacher they wish to mentor. Assigning mentors to new teachers can sometimes backfire because there is a personality clash. If mentors choose who they wish to work with, there usually is greater commitment and fewer problems.

Principals can minimize the obstacles to effective mentoring (Ganser, 1996). Mentoring, when it does happen, may be haphazard at best. Often, the mentoring teacher receives negligible formal training, little or no reduction in his or her workload, and no additional monetary compensation. In many instances, it is an unpaid, thankless "duty." The quality of mentoring in school settings often depends on the ability of the staff to incorporate career development concepts and activities into the curriculum and to consult with and use staff members for beginning teacher improvement.

It is beneficial to work with a committee of both experienced and beginning teachers to establish the goals, objectives, organization, and structure of the mentoring program. To build a successful program, you should:

- Evaluate the need for a mentoring program. Will it help new teachers?
- Identify essential components of effective mentoring programs.
- Decide what the program should accomplish. This can include pedagogy, classroom management, adjustment to the new position, new ideas in teaching, teamwork, and so forth.
- Conclude how it is going to help new teachers.
- Decide how the program will be implemented.
- Set the structure of the program. Will it be a "buddy system," informal/formal, and so forth.
- Determine the cost of the program and how the funds are to be procured.
- Consider the time involved. This can range from minimal to extensive.
- Outline the responsibilities of mentoring teachers, beginning teachers, and administrators. What role does each play? What is expected of the novice teachers? How are the mentors to be selected and trained?
- Evaluate the program. Principals need to constantly review and tweak aspects of the program when needed. Use the force field described in chapter 2 to evaluate during and at the end of the program (Feiman-Nemser, 1996).

Principals play a key role in facilitating the work of experienced teachers who serve as mentors, including preparing them for the role. Veteran teachers may have little experience with the core activity of mentoring—observing and discussing pedagogy with their colleagues. Most teachers, especially those teaching in high schools, often work in isolation with little contact with their peers. This isolation, coupled with the lack of opportunity to observe and discuss each other's work, can be a handicap when working with novices (Little, 1990). Specific suggestions for veteran teachers in developing a successful mentoring relationship include the following four phases:

1. Develop a compatible working relationship with the new teacher inside and outside of school.
2. Mutually determine and agree on the mentor's role.
3. Apply effective mentoring styles and strategies.
4. Disengage the relationship gradually so the beginning teacher will not feel abandoned and will be able to organize appropriate support from colleagues.

Finally, the following areas must be explored and determined before the start of a mentoring program:

- Recruiting and selecting the mentors. What experience, traits, and qualities are you looking for?
- Matching the mentor with the beginner. Should expertise, age, experience, personality, ideology, subject similarities come into play? Is it a one-on-one relationship, or should there be more than one mentor for each new teacher? Can one mentor handle several new teachers? As stated previously, it is best to allow the mentor to choose who they wish to work with.
- Selecting incentives. Are there any, and should there be any?
- Determining class adjustment—time for the mentor to observe the beginner's classroom.
- Agreeing on roles and responsibilities. There should be a clear and concise job description with specific guidelines that have understandable roles and responsibilities for each party.
- Ensuring staff development. Mentors need to have training on how best to accomplish their goals.
- Establishing time commitment. This must be understood by all from the beginning. What is the time commitment for the mentor?

The principal must take a leadership role to ensure the stability and success of the program. There will be issues raised that the principal must clarify, such as how to make sure that the beginning teachers realize that the mentor is a resource not an evaluator, as well as encouraging the mentor's acceptance. The principal may also be required to determine the fine line between being helpful and overbearing. How often should the mentor step in during a school day, and how much advice should be given?

Since the 1970s, mentoring has been a vehicle to improve teacher training. University professors and school administrators alike have high hopes that mentoring that blends the theoretical and the practical will help beginning teachers do a better job in the classroom (Ganser, 1996; Gold, 1996). The scale of mentoring has increased substantially as well throughout the United States. Mentoring can help ensure that beginning teachers mature into successful experienced teachers. Thought should also be given to continuing the mentoring for first- and third-year teachers. Bulach & Berry (2001) found that these teachers were less positive about their school than first-year teachers. They concluded that school administrators tend to forget the needs of these teachers after the first year and this leads to low morale.

STRATEGY 7: USING THE SOCIOGRAM

There is nothing more destructive to a school's climate and culture than a student who comes to school with a weapon with the intent to harm someone. A second event that is very destructive from a student's viewpoint is bullying behavior. Bullying behavior often occurs without the knowledge of the faculty because it occurs when faculty can't see it, that is, in the bathroom, on the field, on the playground, in the hallway, and so on.

School administrators need to make sure they have some method for determining the potential for violence in their building. Bulach (2003) has developed a survey that measures the extent of bullying behavior at a school. It measures the types of bullying, where it occurs, how students feel about their safety, how bullying gets reported, and how faculty respond to bullying behavior. Beane & Bulach (2009) also share information on how to identify bullying behavior. Other than the use of surveys and the tips shared by Bulach and Beane, there is another technique called the "sociogram" that is very effective.

There are various methods that can be used in developing a sociogram. The sociometric test consists simply of asking students who they would like to be if they could be some other student in the group. Another technique would be to write down the name of two to five students in the class they would invite to their birthday party. The responses are then tabulated and graphically represented in a sociogram as shown in Figure 6.1. Examination of the sociogram will disclose those individuals who are isolated from the group and any cliques or subgroups that may have formed and those students who are most popular.

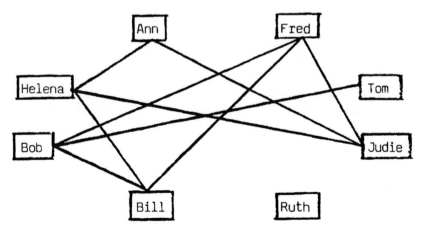

Figure 6.1

A student like Ruth, is an "isolate" and has no friends. As stated in chapter 2, all students have basic human needs: the need to be happy, to feel like life is worth living, to be in control, and to feel cared for. Ruth is a student who has no friends, she probably does not feel in control, does not feel cared for, is not happy, and may be a potential for violence. While it is less frequent that a female brings a gun to school, there is still the potential for violence from someone, whether male of female, who has basic human needs that are not being met. More than likely she is experiencing some form of bullying behavior.

According to Mazzola (2011) "Bullying in our nation's schools is rampant. Consider the following data points from the 2010 Federal Bullying Prevention Summit: every day, 160,000 students stay home out of fear of getting bullied at school; one in three students will be bullied this year (about 18 million young people); 75–80% of all students observe bullying; and, depending on definition, 15–35% of students are victims of cyber-bullying." (p.1)

School administrators must have some method for identifying those students who are "isolates." These students are likely to be bullied and are at risk for failure, dropout, violence, and even suicide. The survey mentioned earlier gives school administrators an overall view of the potential for violence and bullying behavior, but the only way to identify individual students who are at risk is to use some form of the sociogram. More information on the sociogram can be found on the web. Our favorite site is: http://en.wikipedia.org/wiki/Sociogram.

CONCLUSION

Seven specific strategies have been provided to help school principals enhance a school's culture and climate. Each of these strategies also reinforces the concept of servant leadership. Force field analysis is one of the best evaluation tools for obtaining quick and valid data. It can be used to evaluate each of the seven strategies, and it can further enhance the school's culture and climate and reinforce servant leadership. While any one of the seven strategies will enhance a school's climate and culture, the one least used and most valuable is the sociogram. We believe there are many "isolates" in a school, and they are hurting. They do not like school, and do not want to be there. Who is making sure some of their needs are being met? School principals should make identification of "isolates" the number one priority of school counselors.

Principals should also reinforce the redirect process being used at their school with some of these strategies. For example, should volunteers be encouraged to count redirects or should they abstain? Some strategies lend themselves to this process better than others. Certainly, the redirect process being used should be explained at the parent open house.

NOTES

1. Some of the content associated with this strategy is published in the National Association of Secondary School Principals publication *Principal Leadership*, 1(4), (Potter, 2000).

2. Some of the content associated with this strategy is published in the National Association of Secondary School Principals publication *Principal Leadership*, 2(2), (Potter, 1995).

3. Some of the content associated with this strategy is published in the National Association of Secondary School Principal publication *Principal Leadership*, 2(2), (Potter, 2002).

4. Some of the content associated with this strategy is published in a National Association of Secondary School Principal publication *Principal Leadership*, 1(1), (Bulach & Potter, 2000).

5. Some of the content associated with this strategy is published in a National Association of Secondary School Principal publication *Principal Leadership*, 2(8), (Potter, 1999).

6. Some of the content associated with this strategy is published in a National Association of Secondary School Principal publication *Principal Leadership*, 1(2), (Potter, 2000).

REFERENCES

Bulach, C. R., & Potter, L. (2000). How to host a successful open house. *Principal Leadership*, 1(1), 81.

Bulach, C. R., & Berry, J. (2001). The impact of demographic factors on school culture and climate. Paper presented at the Southern Regional Council of Educational Administrators in Jacksonville, FL on 11-3-2001.

Bulach, C. R., Fullbright P. J., & Williams, R. (2003). Bullying behavior: What is the potential for violence at your school? *Journal of Instructional Psychology*, 20(2), 156–184.

Beane, A. & Bulach, C. R. (September, 2009). Tips for helping children who are bullied. *School Climate Matters*, The Center for Social and Emotional Education.

Darling-Hammond, L. (1998). Teacher learning that supports student learning. *Educational Leadership*, 55(5), 6–11.

Feiman-Nemser, S. (1996). *Teacher mentoring: A critical review.* Washington, D.C.: Eric Clearinghouse.

Ganser, T. (1996). Preparing mentors for beginning teachers: An overview for staff development. *Journal of Staff Development,* 17(4), 8–11.

Gold, Y. (1996). Beginning teacher support: Attrition, mentoring, and induction. In J. Sikula, T. J. Buttery, & E. Guyton (Eds.), *Handbook of research on teacher education,* (2nd ed.) (pp. 548–594). New York: Macmillan.

Hanna, J. (1998). School climate: Changing fear to fun. *Contemporary Education,* 69(2), n.p.

Hsiehe, C., & Shen, J. (1998). Teachers', principals', and superintendents' concept of leadership. *School Leadership and Management,* 18(1), n.p.

Lankford, B. A. (1996). *The role of mentoring in career education.* Columbus, OH: Eric Clearinghouse.

Little, J. W. (1990). The mentor phenomenon and the social organization of teaching. *Review of Research Education,* 16(1), n.p.

Mazzola, J. W. (January, 2011) Bullying in schools: A strategic solution. Character Education Partnership, http://www.character.org/uploads/PDFs/Bully Prevention/ BullyinginSchoolsJan192010.pdf

Odell, S. (1990). *Mentoring teacher programs: What research says to the teacher.* Washington, D.C., National Education Association.

Potter, L. (1995, March). How to improve teacher morale: Create a duty-free school. *Principal Leadership,* 2(2), n.p.

Potter, L. (1999, September). How to establish and maintain a volunteer program. *Principal Leadership,* 2(8), n.p.

Potter, L. (2000, February). How to develop a mentoring program for beginning teachers. *Principal Leadership,* 2(2), n.p.

Potter, L. (2000, April). How to improve your school's climate by establishing visibility. *Principal Leadership,* 1(2), n.p.

Richardson, G. D., & Sistrunk, W. E. (1989). The relationship between secondary teachers' perceived levels of burnout and their perceptions of their principals' supervisory behavior. Paper presented at the annual meeting of the Mid-South Educational Research Association, Little Rock, Arkansas.

Part III

Leadership Skills Needed

In parts I and II, the authors share a specific mission and vision for the high-performing school. In part III, they provide additional strategies and techniques to further enhance a school's culture and climate.

Chapter 7

Cultivating Community, Culture, and Learning

We begin this chapter with a brief discussion of the reconceptualization of the role of the principal required in a high-performing school. Next we discuss the ways principals develop the capacity of the people within their schools to function as professional learning communities in a high-performing school. We then examine the elements of school culture that encourage learning for all students and the professional growth of faculty necessary in a high-performing school. Finally, we conclude the chapter with a discussion of the principal's role as instructional leader, the primary focus of which is to promote the learning and success of all students.

REFRAMING THE ROLE OF THE PRINCIPAL

The type of principal needed in a high-performing school calls for a new approach to managing schools. The principal, faculty, staff, parents, and community work together, sharing a vision of how to help all students achieve. Each school is considered a professional learning community. Management is less hierarchical (Lunenburg, 2003; Rubin, 2009). Important decisions are made as much by site-level stakeholders as by state- or district-level participants.

This emerging view of the principalship accounts for the centrality of organic and adaptive models of organization (Kruse & Louis, 2009) and the importance of site-based management. That is, decisions about school programs are decentralized to the school level, and leadership is no longer limited to formal organizational positions (Patronis, 2010). Leadership and management are based on ability rather than role (Smylie, 2010). Leadership activities are dispersed according to competence for required tasks rather than authority.

This altered view of the principalship explains the centrality of the empowerment of teachers, parents, and students; the importance of site-based decision making; and the development of professional learning communities. In a sense, all stakeholders are servants of each other in the true sense of servant leadership. That being said, the reality of the situation is that directives from central office and state departments of education still play a major role in how a principal operates a school.

Stakeholder empowerment, site-based decision making, and professional learning communities, then, are at the very core of a redefinition of the role of the principal in a high-performing school. In high-performing schools, principals clearly define themselves as a servant at the center of the school's staff rather than at the top. Their use of the freeing forms of power is part of their leadership style. Instead of occupying an authoritative position, they prefer to give leadership to others and guide by example and by indirectly inducing thoughtfulness, rather than by making direct suggestions.

In each instance, their role as an authority figure is downplayed, and their role as a source of support and assistance is emphasized, that is, they are servants. These emergent principals believe in delegation, in developing collaborative decision-making processes, and in stepping back from being the chief problem solver in a school by linking these roles more explicitly to the development of a professional learning community (DuFour, DuFour, & Eaker, 2009; Kruse & Louis, 2009; Senge, 2010).

CREATING A PROFESSIONAL LEARNING COMMUNITY

Since their inception, schools have continually sought to improve, whether in response to demands from teachers, administrators, parents, policymakers, or legislators. When we look at the research on improving schools and examine the keys to school improvement, it invariably boils down to the ability of the people within the school to function as a professional learning community (Bowgren & Sever, 2010; Blankstein, Houston, & Cole, 2008; DuFour, DuFour, & Eaker, 2009; Katz, Earl, & Ben Jaafar, 2009; Graham & Ferriter, 2010). A professional learning community shares a vision. That vision was described in chapters 1–5. The philosophy of a professional learning community and servant leadership is collaboration—people working together.

The whole philosophy of a professional learning community is people working together. Each member of the community wants to help the other succeed in daily interactions between staff and principals. All stakeholders—members of the board of education, the superintendent, the faculty, and the support staff—move together to implement this shared vision. Teachers are empowered to do what is best for their students. Involving others in decision-making processes and empowering them to act on their ideas is one of the most significant and effective strategies used by capable leaders (English. 2008; Northouse, 2010). There is an attitude of cooperation and a willingness to serve others as opposed to serving self. There is never fear of asking for help. The support participants working in a professional learning community feel is systemic (Senge, 2010). The ability to explore and ask questions—asking peers and supervisors—is only possible when it comes from the top (Marzano & Waters, 2010).

The principal is the key player in creating this community. The role he or she plays is a vital one. The principal begins by bringing the faculty together in a four step process: a) reinforcing the mission, b) reinforcing the vision, c) developing value statements, and d) establishing goals (DuFour, DuFour, & Eaker, 2009; DuFour, DuFour, & Many, 2007; DuFour & Eaker, 1998; DuFour, Eaker, & DuFour, 2006). Each will be discussed in turn.

Reinforcing the Mission

The mission of creating a high performing school culture described in the first five chapters drives the day-to-day teaching and learning that takes place in the school. The principal must engage the faculty in a deeper discussion; for example, why do we exist? The typical response will be that we exist to help all students learn. For example, successful professional learning communities believe that all students can learn. That statement will only become meaningful if the faculty is willing to engage in some deeper questions. For example, if we believe that all students can learn, we expect them to learn. How will faculty respond when students do not learn (DuFour & Eaker, 2005; DuFour, DuFour, Eaker, & Karhanek, 2010)? What does it mean to help students learn how to learn? That goes beyond reading and mathematics to how do students organize their time and materials? How do they work together (Bellanca & Brandt, 2010)?

A professional learning community involves all stakeholders working together, including students. What kind of skills do students need to work together, to control each other, to reduce redirects, and to reduce bullying behavior? What kind of skills do they need to understand themselves, to identify their own learning style, and to evaluate themselves? How good are they at applying their learning to other contexts both inside and outside the school? And how do students use technology and other resources to learn on their own?

Reinforcing the Vision

After reinforcing the school's mission, the next step is to reinforce the vision. In a high-performing school, students have a lot of control over the behavior of the other students. They are encouraged to control their own behavior and the behavior of the other students through use of the redirects. They discourage bullying behavior and intervene when they see it. Additionally, they (a) accept responsibility for their learning, decisions, and actions; (b) develop skills to become more self-directed learners as they progress through the grades; and (c) actively engage in and give effort to academic and extracurricular pursuits (DuFour, DuFour, & Eaker, 2009; Lunenburg & Ornstein, 2012).

Professional learning community advocates recommend several tips for reinforcing the vision for your school (DuFour, DuFour, Eaker, & Many, 2007; Graham & Ferriter, 2010). Engage the faculty in a general agreement about what they hope their school will become. Enlist a faculty task force to identify what works and does not work with the system of redirects described in chapter 1 and share the findings with the rest of the faculty. Conduct small group discussion sessions that enable the faculty to review these findings. Discussions could also include criticisms of the traditional structure and culture of schools.

A traditional obstacle for schools hoping to move forward is the inherent tradition of teacher isolation in schools (Elmore, 2005; Senge, 2010). This must be addressed and overcome for a school to become a professional learning community. At all levels of the system, isolation is seen as the enemy of school improvement (Fullan, 2010a). Thus, most day-to-day activities need to be specifically designed to connect teachers, principals, and district administrators with one another and with outside experts.

If at this point, the principal is still not sure about what the faculty wants for their school, force field analysis described in chapter 2 can be utilized. For example, the following two sentences can produce a clearer picture of what the faculty desires (complete these two sentences as often as you wish):

I like working at our school because . . . (forces for)
I would like working at our school better if . . . (forces against)

The force field analysis process addresses both the positive and negative aspects of what is happening at the school and can sometimes provide a clearer vision of what the faculty wants for their school. The same process can be used for students and parents with a slight change in wording.

It should be noted that while the principal remains a valued participant in reinforcing the vision, vision is embodied by the process rather than by individuals (Kruse & Louis, 2009). Principals must help keep their colleagues from narrowing their vision and assist the school in maintaining "a broader perspective" (Fullan, 2010b). Excellence is a moving target; therefore, the vision should be revisited periodically to ensure that it remains relevant. Principals, in a sense, are keepers of the vision. The principal's modeling and reinforcing of vision-related behaviors are crucial to the success of the professional learning community (DuFour, Eaker, & DuFour, 2006).

Developing Value Statements

The next stage in the process is to develop value statements. At this point, the members of another faculty task force might begin to work with their colleagues to identify shared values. For example, how do they feel about the character education plan described in chapter 5? What character trait will be the focus next year? The attitudes, behaviors, and commitments of all teachers need to be identified and demonstrated so as to reinforce the vision and mission.

The board of education, support staff, administrative team, students, parents, and community members should also engage in discussions about the attitudes, behaviors, and commitments the school needs from them to advance the vision. For example, what attitudes, behaviors, and commitments must the board of education promise to enable the school to achieve the vision? What attitudes, behaviors, and commitments must the parents promise to become contributors to creating the school described in the vision? The process continues until all stakeholders are considered.

DuFour and colleagues (2009) recommended a process for developing shared value statements. Each group begins by examining the vision and identifying what they must do to reinforce it. For example, what can the board of education, superintendent, principal, teachers, parents, and students do to advance the school toward the vision? Each group should work in two teams of five. When all the ideas are listed, the five members review each individual idea. The ideas are shared between the two teams in each group.

All ideas generated are then broken down into four, five, or six general themes or categories. The groups do not need to have hundreds of value statements. A handful of value statements is most effective. Throughout this process, it is more powerful to articulate behaviors than beliefs. It is more important that each group express what they are prepared to do than what they believe.

The challenge for each group as they go through the process is to get them to understand that they need to focus on themselves. They should ask, what attitudes, behaviors, and commitments are we individually prepared to pledge to move this school forward? After every group engages in this discussion, each should articulate the commitments they are prepared to make. At this point, the faculty has reached its first important milestone in the improvement process and can become more specific in terms of where they go from there.

Establishing Goals

To achieve the school's vision, stakeholders must establish goals based on the adopted value statements. Goals are the results the faculty tries to achieve (Locke & Latham, 1995). This definition implies at least three relationships between goals and the principal.

First, in terms of laying a foundation for a professional learning community, goals represent the implementation phase of school improvement. The determination of school goals is a primary responsibility of principals. In a professional learning community, faculty members are active and valued participants in establishing goals with the principal and other stakeholders. Goals become guideposts in defining standards of school improvement efforts. Without clearly stated goals, no means exist to determine if acceptable standards of school improvement have been met (Lunenburg & Ornstein, 2012).

Second, goals are influenced by the aspirations of a school district's key administrators (Marzano & Waters, 2010). For example, the goal of a school to be connected to the Internet, to have a computer lab in every school, to have computers in every classroom, and to provide professional development for faculty assumes that the district has or can obtain adequate resources to achieve the goal and that the goal is desired by the top administrators of the school district. This is more likely to happen in a professional learning community since all stakeholders were involved in developing a mission statement, vision, values, and goals.

Third, goals reflect a desired end result of school actions—what they wish to accomplish. It is important when formulating goals that we don't confuse means with ends (DuFour, DuFour, & Eaker, 2009). A powerful goal, and an appropriate one for school improvement, would be that "every student in the school will be reading at grade level by third grade." It is direct. It is stating exactly what you want to accomplish. It is measurable. It is an end. It should be noted that because the vision is rather broad and tends to point to lots of different areas in the school, the principal and faculty are not going to be able to attack every area at once. There has to be some decision about which areas take priority (Foster, 2008). In a high performing school culture, the role of reducing redirects is a primary goal. The faculty should set and reset the benchmark or goal for students to achieve the reward. Is the goal for redirects a daily or a weekly goal?

The focus may need to be narrowed, and goals help to narrow the focus. Principals can provide a faculty with parameters for identifying goals that directly impact implementing the high performing school concept. A caring and cooperative learning environment has to be the focus. The process of implementing the redirects and servant leadership activities should help to achieve the stated goals. Goals, however, should be explicit and measurable. Some examples of explicit measurable goals are the following:

- There will be a one percent improvement in standardized test scores.
- There will be a one percent improvement in school culture and climate scores.
- There will be a one percent improvement in student character behavior scores.
- There will be a one percent improvement in attendance.
- There will be a one percent improvement in the student graduation rate.
- There will be a one percent decrease in the number of students assigned to the alternative education program.
- There will be a one percent improvement in the student dropout rate.
- There will be a one percent decrease in tardies.
- There will be a one percent decrease in office referrals.
- There will be a one percent improvement in teacher turnover.
- There will be a ten percent reduction in the number of redirects.

The presence of explicit goals benefits all stakeholders by fostering commitment, providing performance standards and targets, and enhancing motivation (Wallach, 2008).

- Commitment: Goal statements describe the school's purpose to participants. The process of getting participants to agree to pursue a specific goal gives those individuals a personal stake in the outcome. Thus, goals are helpful in encouraging personal commitment to collective ends.
- Standards: Because goals define desired outcomes for the school, they also serve as performance criteria. When appraising performance, principals need goals as an established standard against which they can measure performance. Clearly defined goals enable principals to weigh performance objectively on the basis of accomplishment rather than subjectively on the basis of personality. For example, if a school wishes to increase test scores by one percent and the actual increase is five percent, the principal and faculty have exceeded the prescribed standard.

- Targets: School goals provide principals with specific targets and direct collegial efforts toward given outcomes. People tend to pursue their own ends in the absence of formal organizational goals.
- Motivation: In addition to serving as targets, standards, and commitment, goals perform a role in encouraging colleagues to perform at their highest levels. Moreover, goals give principals a rational basis for rewarding performance. If colleagues receive rewards equal to their levels of performance, they will continue to exert high levels of effort.

To make the school's mission, vision, values, and goals something more than words on paper, the principal needs to communicate and model them so that they are embedded in daily school life. The principal is the keeper of the vision and the one who keeps articulating it, and when people are at the point where they say they can't go anymore, the principal is the one who reminds them of why they can do it. It is repeating messages over and over again. It is reminding people where they started, where they are now, and where they are headed. This is done in a variety of different venues: Writing about it in the weekly newsletter and talking about it at parent teacher organizations and faculty meetings so that the school community sees the way business is conducted at the school.

That's important but it's not enough. What is necessary is day-to-day work. When a principal sits down with a faculty member to talk about a lesson observed, he or she may bring up the vision and how the lesson connects to that vision. The principal may bring up the vision when discussing the budget with faculty. When the principal is hiring faculty or making faculty changes, or if he or she is engaged in curriculum changes or implementing new courses, the vision is always used as the filter.

When the principal acts in such a way, the people involved in a professional learning community will see the importance of the vision. Thus, the principal, as a change agent, works with the faculty to create new programs and procedures that evolve from the shared vision and goals.

To develop this culture for the vision that has been created, the existing culture must be identified. The expectations diagnosis (described in chapter 2) should be utilized to identify what the faculty values and expects in terms of attitudes, behaviors, and commitments. It is difficult to develop a plan to achieve a new culture if you have not identified the old one.

Maintaining School Culture

In a high-performing school, principals work with all stakeholders to maintain the culture. The expectations diagnosis and force field analysis are great tools for involving everyone. Maintaining a school's culture is a conscious endeavor, and principals must be proactive as they go about doing so. They begin by having people articulate in very specific terms the kinds of behaviors and commitments they think are necessary to move their school forward. This is a challenge, for every school faces the issue of maintaining school culture. Once the high performing school culture is created, a number of mechanisms help solidify the acceptance of the values and ensure that the culture is maintained or reinforced (organizational socialization). These mechanisms are the following steps for socializing employees (Kruse & Louis, 2009).

Step 1: Hiring Staff

The socialization process starts with the careful selection of employees. Trained recruiters use standardized procedures and focus on values that are important in the culture. Those candidates whose personal values do not fit with the underlying values of the school are given ample opportunity to opt out (deselect).

Step 2: Orientation

After the chosen candidate is hired, considerable training ensues to expose the person to the culture. Many forms of orientation are also provided to incoming students, for example, transitions from elementary school to middle school and middle school to high school.

Step 3: Job Mastery

Whereas Step 2 is intended to foster cultural learning, Step 3 is designed to develop the employee's technological knowledge. As employees move along a career path, the organization assesses their performance and assigns other responsibilities on the basis of their progress. Frequently, schools establish a step-by-step approach to this career plan. For example, some groups recommend a three-step career ladder process for teachers: (a) instructors, (b) professional teachers, and (c) career professionals. Other groups propose four steps: (a) licensed teachers, (b) certified teachers, (c) advanced certified teachers, and (d) lead teachers.

Step 4: Establishing Reward and Control Systems

The school pays meticulous attention to measuring results and rewarding individual performance. Reward systems are comprehensive, are consistent, and focus on those aspects of the school that are tied to success and the values of the culture. For example, school officials will specify the factors that are considered important for success. Operational measures are used to assess these factors, and performance appraisals of employees are tied to the accomplishment of these factors.

Promotion and merit pay are determined by success on each of the predetermined critical factors. For example, teachers who do not want to use the redirects and fit the school's culture are transferred to another school or are dismissed. It should be noted that collective bargaining agreements may stipulate procedures for teacher transfer or grounds for dismissal (American Arbitration Association, 2010).

Step 5: Adhering to Values

As personnel continue to work for the school, their behavior closely matches the underlying values of the culture. Identification with underlying values helps employees reconcile personal sacrifices caused by their membership to the school. Personnel learn to accept the school's values and place their trust in school personnel not to hurt them. For instance, teachers work long hours on a multiplicity of fragmented tasks for which they sometimes receive little recognition from their superiors, their subordinates, and the community. They sometimes endure ineffective school board members and supervisors and job assignments that are undesirable and inconvenient. Identification with the common values of the school allows these teachers to justify such personal sacrifices.

Step 6: Reinforcing Folklore

Throughout the socialization process, the school exposes its members to rites and rituals, stories or myths, and heroes or heroines that portray and reinforce the culture. For example, in one educational institution the story is told of a principal who was fired because of his harsh handling of teachers. The principal had incorrectly believed a myth that being tough with his teachers would enhance himself in the eyes of his superiors. The school district deemed such leadership behavior to be inconsistent with its school district philosophy of cultivating good interpersonal relationships and high levels of morale and job satisfaction among all its employees.

Step 7: Identifying Consistent Role Models

Those individuals who have performed well serve as role models and mentors to newcomers. By identifying these teachers as symbolizing success, the school encourages others to do likewise. Role models in strong-culture schools can be thought of as one type of ongoing staff development for all teachers.

* * *

As developers of culture, principals ensure that their school's culture reflects its vision and values. They do this by engaging all members of the faculty and staff. Together they reflect on what they value and envision and how they will act to support those values. They regularly audit their culture. They orient new staff and incoming students. They recognize heroes and heroines, share stories, and celebrate people whose contributions reinforce the culture. There are many things teachers can do to help facilitate the culture of a building, but there has to be a leader—the principal—who is willing to absorb and buy into the culture and climate to make a difference. Without that leader, the school will not have a very positive culture.

Every school has a culture whether it is being attended to or not. If a school does nothing to maintain the culture, it will create itself. Students will create it. Faculty will create it. Students will create their little piece of the culture. Teachers will create their little piece of the culture. Support staff will create their little piece of the culture. Ultimately, there will be a school culture. As described in chapter 2, the underlying culture will create the school's climate. Will everyone be moving in the same direction with that culture? Will all stakeholders share the same mission, vision, values, and goals? Not likely.

In a high-performing school, principals work with all stakeholders to develop the culture. Culture is a conscious endeavor, and principals must be proactive as they go about creating a culture that is advancing the school toward its vision and reinforcing the behaviors necessary for moving the school forward. Throughout the development of a school culture, student achievement must be paramount. A school should be a place where students come to learn. Principals can make that happen by functioning as instructional leaders while reinforcing and maintaining the culture for a high performing school.

THE PRINCIPAL AS INSTRUCTIONAL LEADER

Demands for greater accountability, especially appeals for the use of more outcome-based measures, require the principal to be instruction oriented. Is the redirect process improving time on task in each classroom? Are the students learning? If the students are not learning, what are we going to do about it? The focus on results, student achievement, and higher levels of learning can only happen if teaching and learning become the central focus of the school and the principal (Blankstein, 2010).

How can principals help teachers clarify instructional goals and work collaboratively to improve teaching and learning to meet those goals? Principals need to help teachers shift their focus from what they are teaching to what students are learning. We cannot continue to accept the premise; I taught it, they just didn't learn it. The role of instructional leader helps the school maintain a focus on why the school exists. The school exists to help all students learn (Blasé, Blasé, & Phillips, 2010; Smylie, 2010).

The principal needs to shift the focus of instruction from teaching to learning and create collaborative structures and processes for faculty to work together to improve instruction. Professional development must be ongoing and focused on the school mission. These are among the key tasks that principals must perform to be effective instructional leaders in a high-performing school. School principals can accomplish this by (a) focusing on learning, (b) encouraging collaboration, (c) analyzing results, (d) providing support, and (e) aligning curriculum, instruction, and assessment. Together, these five dimensions provide a compelling framework for accomplishing sustained success for all children (Fullan, 2010a; Lunenburg, 2003; Marzano & Waters, 2010). It is helpful if there is district wide leadership focused directly on learning; however, principals can be successful in shifting the focus from teaching to learning even if it does not exist at the district level.

Focusing on Learning

Principals can help shift the focus from teaching to learning if they insist that certain critical questions be considered, and principals are in a key position to pose those questions (DuFour, DuFour, & Eaker, 2009). How can we continue to reduce student misbehavior and increase time on task? Is the redirect process working? What do we want our students to know and be able to do? The focus in a high-performing school is not on are you teaching but rather are the students learning? How will you know if the students are learning? How will we respond when students do not learn? What criteria will we use to evaluate student progress? How can we more effectively use the time and resources available to help students learn? How can we engage parents in helping our students learn? Have we established systematic collaboration as the norm in our school?

Encouraging Collaboration

A key task for principals is to create a collective expectation among teachers concerning student performance. That is, principals need to raise the collective sense of teachers about student learning (DuFour, DuFour, Eaker, & Karhanek, 2010). Then principals must work to ensure that teacher expectations are aligned with the school's instructional goals. Furthermore, principals need to eliminate teacher isolation so that discussions about student learning become a collective mission of the school (Elmore, 2005; Senge, 2010).

Principals must develop and sustain school structures and cultures that foster individual and group learning. That is, principals must stimulate an environment in which new information and practices are eagerly incorporated into the system. Teachers are more likely to pursue group and individual learning when there are supportive conditions in the school, such as particularly effective leadership (English, 2008; Northouse, 2010). Schools where teachers collaborate in discussing issues related to student learning are more likely to be able to take advantage of internally and externally generated information. Teachers can become willing recipients of research information if they are embedded in a setting where meaningful and sustained interaction with researchers occurs in an egalitarian context (Blankstein, Houston, & Cole, 2009).

One popular collaboration structure is teacher teams. Schools are recognizing that teachers should be working together in teams as opposed to working individually in isolation in their classrooms. High-performing teams accomplish six things (Smylie, 2010):

1. They clarify what students should know and are able to do as a result of each unit of instruction. If teachers are clear on the intended results of instruction, they are more effective.
2. They design curriculum and share instructional strategies to achieve those outcomes.
3. They develop valid assessment strategies that measure how well students are performing.
4. They analyze the results and work together to come up with new ideas for improving those results. Regular assessment and analysis of student learning are key parts of the team's process.
5. They compare how the redirects are working and what they can do to improve the process.
6. They discuss how the nine forms of power (chapter 4) are being used to move students from a level of dependence to one of independence.

Analyzing Results

How can schools gauge their progress with achieving student learning? Three factors can increase a school's progress in achieving learning for all students (Blankstein, Houston, & Cole, 2010; Love, 2009). The primary factor is the availability of performance data connected to each student. Performance data need to be broken down by specific objectives and target levels in the school curriculum. Then the school is able to connect what is taught to what is learned.

The curriculum goals should be clear enough to specify what each teacher should teach. The assessment measure must be aligned with the curriculum for a valid measure of what students have learned (Popham, 2010a; 2010b). Teachers also need access to longitudinal data on each student in their classroom. With such data, they are able to develop individual and small-group education plans to ensure mastery of areas of weakness from previous years while also moving students forward in the school curriculum.

The second factor is the public nature of the assessment system. The school district should publish an annual matrix of schools and honor those schools that have performed at high levels. This provides role models for other schools to emulate. At the school and classroom levels, it provides a blueprint of those areas where teachers should focus their individual education plans (IEPs) and where grade levels or schools should focus the school's professional development plans.

The public nature of the data from the accountability system makes clear where schools are. Data should be disaggregated by race/ethnicity, socioeconomic status, English language proficiency, and disability. Performance of each subgroup of students on assessment measures makes the school community aware of which students are well served and which students are not well served by the school's curriculum and instruction.

The third factor, in gauging progress with achieving student learning, is the specifically targeted assistance provided to students who are performing at low levels. Teachers learn how to develop an improvement plan to guide their activities and monitor the outcomes of the activities, all of which are designed to raise student performance levels.

Once a team of teachers has worked together and identified students who are having difficulty, the school faces the challenge of responding to the students who are not learning (DuFour, DuFour, Eaker, & Karhanek, 2010). The challenge is not simply reteaching the same way teachers taught before but providing support for teachers to expand their repertoire of skills and providing support and time for students to get the additional assistance they need to master those skills. When students are not learning, principals must ensure that professional development programs are in place to give additional support to teachers and make certain that intervention strategies are in place to give additional support to students (Joyce & Calhoun, 2010).

Providing Support

Teachers need to be provided with the training, teaching tools, and support they need to help all students reach high-performance levels. Specifically, teachers need access to curriculum guides, textbooks, and/or specific training connected to the school curriculum. They need access to lessons or teaching units that match curriculum goals. They need training on using assessment results to diagnose learning gaps (Downey, Steffy, Poston, & English, 2009). Teachers must know how each student performed on every multiple-choice item and other questions on the assessment measure. And training must be in the teachers' subject areas. Only then can they be prepared to help students achieve at high levels.

In addition to professional development for teachers, all schools need an intervention and support system for students who lag behind in learning the curriculum. Schools need to provide additional help to students who lag behind in core subjects either in school, after school, on weekends, or during the summer. Boards of education and school superintendents need to supply the financial resources to fulfill this mandate. This involves acquiring materials, information, or technology; manipulating schedules or release time to create opportunities for teachers to learn; facilitating professional networks; and creating an environment that supports school improvement efforts (Lunenburg & Ornstein, 2012).

A focus on student learning usually means changes in curriculum, instruction, and assessment—that is, changes in teaching. The history of school reform indicates that innovations in teaching and learning seldom penetrate more than a few schools and seldom endure when they do (Elmore, 2005). Innovations frequently fail because the teachers—those closest to the firing line—who make it happen may not be committed to the effort or may not have the skills to grapple with the basic challenge at hand (Fullan, Hill, & Crevola, 2006; Fullan & St. Germain, 2006). Principals need to ensure that teachers have the skills to help all students perform at high levels.

Aligning Curriculum, Instruction, and Assessment

Principals need to ensure that assessment of student learning is aligned with both the school's curriculum and the teachers' instruction (English, 2000; Popham, 2010a). When assessments are well constructed and implemented, changes in the nature of teaching and learning will occur. Aligning assessment with teaching and learning can lead to a richer, more challenging curriculum; foster discussion and collaboration among teachers within and across schools; create more productive conversations among teachers and parents; and focus stakeholders' attention on increasing student achievement.

For curriculum goals to have an impact on what happens in classrooms, they must be clear. When school districts, administrators, and students are held accountable for results, more specificity is needed in implementing the curriculum. In a high-stakes accountability environment, teachers require that the curriculum contain enough detail and precision to allow them to know what the students need to learn (Schiro, 2007).

High-performing schools attempt to align their assessment measures with their curriculum. Lunenburg and Ornstein (2012) encouraged schools to consider three principles in this endeavor. First, assessments not based on the curriculum are neither fair nor helpful to parents or students. Schools that have developed their own assessment measures have done a good job of ensuring that the content of the assessment can be found in the curriculum. That is, children will not be assessed on knowledge and skills they have not been taught. This is what English (2000) referred to as "the doctrine of no surprises." However, the same is not true when schools use generic, off-the-shelf standardized tests. Such tests cannot measure the breadth and depth of the school's curriculum.

Second, when the curriculum is rich and rigorous, the assessments must be as well. Assessments must tap both the breadth and depth of the content and skills in the curriculum. Third, assessments must become more challenging in each successive grade. The solid foundation of knowledge and skills developed in early grades should evolve into more complex skills in later grades.

If one accepts the premise that assessment drives curriculum and instruction, perhaps the easiest way to improve instruction and increase student achievement is to construct better assessments (Popham, 2010a, 2010b; Yeh, 2001). According to Yeh, it is possible to design forced-choice items (multiple-choice items) that test reasoning and critical thinking. Such assessments could require students to use facts, rather than recall them. And questions could elicit content knowledge that is worth learning.

To prepare students to think critically, teachers could teach children to identify what is significant. Teachers can model the critical thinking process in the classroom, during instruction, through assignments, in preparing for assessments, and in the content of the assessment itself. By aligning content with worthwhile questions in core subject areas, it may be possible to rescue assessment and instruction from the current focus on the recall of trivial factual knowledge. Assessment items could be created for a range of subjects and levels of difficulty. Then there would be little incentive for teachers to drill students on factual knowledge.

CONCLUSION

The role of the principal has changed from a hierarchical, bureaucratic image to one of servant leadership, shared decision making, and school self-determination. Principals need to champion the redirect process and focus on continually lowering the number of times teachers stop teaching to correct student behavior. Increased time on task will foster a high-performing school culture, and promote student learning and test scores. This will also improve the capacity of his or her staff to function as a professional learning community and his or her students to function as good citizens upon graduation. Developing and maintaining a positive school culture cultivates a high-performing school, the learning and success of all students, and the professional growth of faculty. The instructional leadership of the principal is a critical factor in developing a high-performing school. The primary responsibility of the principal is to work with faculty to create a school culture that creates a caring learning environment and promotes the learning and success of all students. The end result will be higher test scores, reduced dropout rate, and reduced bullying behavior.

REFERENCES

American Arbitration Association (2010). *An inside look at collective bargaining.* New York, NY: The Author.

Bellanca, J., & Brandt, R. (2010). *21st century skills: Rethinking how students learn.* Bloomington, IN: Solution Tree.

Blankstein, A. M. (2010). *Failure is not an option: 6 principles for making student success the only option* (2nd ed.). Thousand Oaks, CA: Sage.

Blankstein, A. M., Houston, P. D., & Cole, R. W. (2008). *Sustaining professional learning communities.* Thousand Oaks, CA: Corwin Press.

Blankstein, A. M., Houston, P. D., Cole, R. W. (2009). *Building sustainable leadership capacity.* Thousand Oaks, CA: Corwin Press.

Blankstein, A. M., Houston, P. D., & Cole, R. W. (2010). *Data enhanced leadership.* Thousand Oaks, CA: Corwin Press.

Blase, J., Blase, J., & Phillips, D. Y. (2010). *Handbook of school improvement: How high-performing principals create high-performing schools.* Thousand Oaks, CA: Corwin Press.

Bowgren, L., & Sever, K. (2010). *Differential professional development in a professional learning community.* Thousand Oaks, CA: Corwin Press.

Downey, C. J., Steffy, B. E., Poston, W. K., & English, F. W. (2009). *50 ways to close the achievement gap* (3rd ed.). Thousand Oaks, CA: Corwin Press.

DuFour, R., DuFour, R., & Eaker, R. (2009). *Revisiting professional learning communities at work: New insights for improving schools.* Bloomington, IN: Solution Tree.

DuFour, R., Dufour, R., Eaker, R., & Karhanek, G. (2010). *Raising the bar and closing the gap whatever it takes.* Bloomington, IN: Solution Tree.

DuFour, R., DuFour, R., Eaker, R., & Many, T. (2007). *Learning by doing: A handbook for professional learning communities at work.* Bloomington, IN: Solution Tree.

DuFour, R., & & Eaker, R. (2005). *Whatever it takes: How professional learning communities respond when kids don't learn.* Bloomington, IN: Solution Tree.

DuFour, R., & Eaker, R. (1998). *Professional learning communities at work: Best practices for enhancing student achievement.* Bloomington, IN: Solution Tree.

DuFour, R., Eaker, R., & DuFour, R. (2006). On *common ground: The power of professional learning communities.* Bloomington, IN: Solution Tree.

Elmore, R. F. (2005). *School reform from the inside out: Policy, practice, and performance.* Boston, MA: Harvard Education Publishing Group.

English, F. W. (2000). *Deciding what to teach and test: Developing, aligning, and auditing the curriculum.* Thousand Oaks, CA: Corwin Press.

English, F. W. (2008). *The art of educational leadership: Balancing performance and accountability.* Thousand Oaks, CA: Sage.

Foster, G. (2009). *Working together to improve literacy: How to set goals, implement and assess school-wide reading and writing initiatives.* Stenhouse Publishers.

Fullan, M. (2010a). *All systems go: The change imperative for whole system reform.* Thousand Oaks, CA: Corwin Press.

Fullan, M. (2010b). *Motion leadership: The skinny on becoming change savvy.* Thousand Oaks, CA: Corwin Press.

Fullan, M., Hill, P., Crevola, C. (2006), *Breakthrough.* Thousand Oaks, CA: Corwin Press.

Fullan, & St. Germain, C. (2006). *Learning places: A field guide for improving the schooling.* Thousand Oaks, CA: Corwin Press.

Graham, P., & Ferriter, W. M. (2010). *Building a professional learning community at work: A guide to the first year.* Bloomington, IN: Solution Tree.

Joyce, B, & Calhoun, E. (2010). *Models of professional development: A celebration of educators.* Thousand Oaks, CA: Corwin Press.

Katz, S., Earl, L. M., & Ben Jaafar, S. (2009). *Building and connecting learning communities: The power of networks for school improvement.* Thousand Oaks, CA: Corwin Press.

Kruse, S. D., & Louis, K. S. (2009). *Building strong school cultures: A guide to leading change.* Thousand Oaks, CA: Corwin Press.

Locke, E. E., & Latham, G. P. (1995). *A theory of goal setting and task performance.* Englewood Cliffs, NJ: Prentice Hall.

Love, N. (2009). *Using data to improve learning: A collaborative inquiry.* Thousand Oaks, CA: Corwin Press.

Lunenburg, F. C. (2003). The post-behavioral science era: Excellence, community, and justice. In F. C. Lunenburg & C. S. Carr (Eds.), *Shaping the future: Policy, partnerships, and emerging perspectives* (pp. 36–55). Lanham, MD: Rowman & Littlefield.

Lunenburg, F. C., & Ornstein, A. O. (2012). *Educational administration: Concepts and Practices* (6th ed.). Belmont, CA: Cengage/Wadsworth.

Marzano, R. J., & Waters, T. (2010). *District leadership that works: Striking the right balance.* Bloomington, IN: Solution Tree.

Northouse, P. G. (2010). *Leadership: Theory and practice* (5th ed.). Thousand Oaks, CA: Sage.

Patronis, H. A. (2010). *Decentralized decision making in schools: The theory and evidence on school-based management.* Washington, DC: World Bank Publications.

Popham, W. J. (2010a). *Educational assessment: What school leaders need to know.* ThousandOaks, CA: Corwin Press.

Popham, W. J. (2010b). *Classroom assessment: What teachers need to know.* Upper Saddle River, NJ: Prentice Hall.

Rubin, H. (2009). *Collaborative leadership: Developing effective partnerships for communities and schools* (2nd ed.). Thousand Oaks, CA: Corwin Press.

Schiro, M. S. (2007). Curriculum theory: Conflicting visions and enduring concerns. Thousand Oaks, CA: Sage Publications.

Senge, P. M. (2010). *Schools that learn.* New York: Doubleday.

Smylie, M. A. (2010). *Continuous school improvement.* Thousand Oaks, CA: Corwin Press.

Wallach, G. P. (2009). *Language intervention for school-age students: Setting goals for academic success.* Elsevier.

Yeh, S. S. (2001). Tests worth teaching to: Constructing state-mandated tests that emphasize critical thinking. *Educational Researcher, 30,* 12–17.

Chapter 8

Professional Development

The implementation of any reform, like a high-performing school, requires professional development. Professional development is directly related to improved practice for teachers. No reform can take place without a purposeful, coherent, focused, and sustained system that includes professional development. There are two missions of the principal related to professional development. First, there is the mission the principal must accomplish as it relates to the teachers' professional growth. The second is acting as facilitator of improved teacher—student relations in the classroom as it relates to the creation of a high-performing school. Both of these missions should yield subsequent increases in student achievement, a reduction in bullying behavior, and dropouts.

The first part of the principal's twofold mission is to plan, with teachers, a comprehensive professional development program targeted at identified individual and collective needs. The second part of the mission is to provide resources, including time and money, and to include time for teachers to reflect upon and participate in a dialogue about their practice as it pertains to student learning. Darling-Hammond (2007) made a strong argument for quality professional development by stating that each dollar spent on improving teachers' qualifications nets greater gains in student learning than any other use of an education dollar.

The National Staff Development Council (2007) called for a shift in the way that principals approach professional development. When the council's recommendations include devoting a full 10 percent of the school budget and 25 percent of teacher time to professional development, a general gauge for spending education dollars in professional development is considered to be the following: With 80 percent of a school budget being spent on personnel, it appears that a district and/or campus, in a most conservative way, would spend at least 10 percent of the remaining 20 percent on professional development. With either level of funding, principals must monitor the professional development and demand a return on the public's money. Any practitioner will quickly realize that 10 percent of the budget for professional development is going to be difficult, but it is a target. In many school districts, less than 2 percent is devoted to professional development. Any movement toward 10 percent is an improvement.

There is professional development at the district, school, and individual level. There should be some money earmarked for professional development at the individual level. For example, what if a Title I teacher wants to attend the National Title I conference. What if the reading teacher wanted to attend the National Reading conference? Some of the most meaningful professional development is at the individual level. For those districts with collective bargaining contracts, the amount set aside for professional development and the procedures for using it should be part of the contract. It is a carrot that can be used at the bargaining table to get rid of some of the things the union is trying to get in the contract.

While professional development programs have a long history, present practices have many shortcomings and have not been well received by teachers (Bubb, 2007). The major reason for such lack of enthusiasm by teachers is that professional development programs are often too bureaucratic and centralized with too much emphasis on administrative planning and little input from teachers (Witmer, 2007). Professional development programs and activities are typically designed to present information, help teachers understand this information, help teachers apply this understanding in their teaching, and help teachers accept and be committed to a new approach (Sergiovanni & Starratt, 2006).

Frequently, only knowledge, comprehension, and application are the focus of professional development programs. Accepting and becoming committed to a new approach, such as implementation of a high-performing school, usually requires an attitude change on the part of teachers. A professional development technique called the "We Agree" workshop focuses on changing values and attitudes of staff.

A MODEL FOR PROFESSIONAL DEVELOPMENT

Once the staff has agreed to improve learning in their school by implementing a high-performing school culture, the principal may arrange to have the faculty participate as a group in a "We Agree" workshop. The "We Agree" process is considered basic to the implementation of a new program. Within the framework of planned activities, staff members have an opportunity to examine their own and their colleagues' beliefs concerning issues in education. Through the "We Agree" process, the faculty will use communication skills that will build consensus among all participants concerning their beliefs about such issues as to how students learn, school organization, parent involvement, the role of the teacher, curriculum, and other school concerns that constitute a common philosophical basis for action.

Lunenburg and associates (2001), at the Center for Research and Doctoral Studies in Educational Leadership at Sam Houston State University, developed an Instructional Programming Model (IPM). This model outlines the steps involved in a learning program designed to meet the individual needs of students. Faculty and school administrators will find this conceptualization useful as a guideline for implementing the high-performing school program. The model is presented in Figure 8.1.

The "We Agree" workshop has two major components. The first component further develops the high-performing school culture and consists of a number of activities to facilitate that process. The second component deals with the mechanics involved in implementing a high-performing school culture in a school or school district.

PROFESSIONAL DEVELOPMENT ACTIVITIES

The activities that follow are recommended for the first component of the "We Agree" workshop. Eight activities are presented. The overall collective purpose of the activities is the development of trust. If a reform is to be successfully implemented, a degree of trust has to be established. The development of trust can be enhanced by having faculty examine their own beliefs and their colleagues' beliefs regarding important educational issues and reaching consensus among the faculty on these issues. Trust development requires a degree of openness between faculty members. According to Bulach (2003) openness has a telling and a listening dimension and trust has five dimensions. The five trust dimensions are the following: confidentiality, predictability, truthfulness, character, and ability.

The activities are presented in a sequence and numbered consecutively. All activities require faculty to use the telling and listening dimensions of openness which will lead to the development of trust. Not all activities need to be used with all groups, but the sequence of activities should be followed as presented. Other activities may be added or substituted for those listed at the discretion of the workshop facilitator.

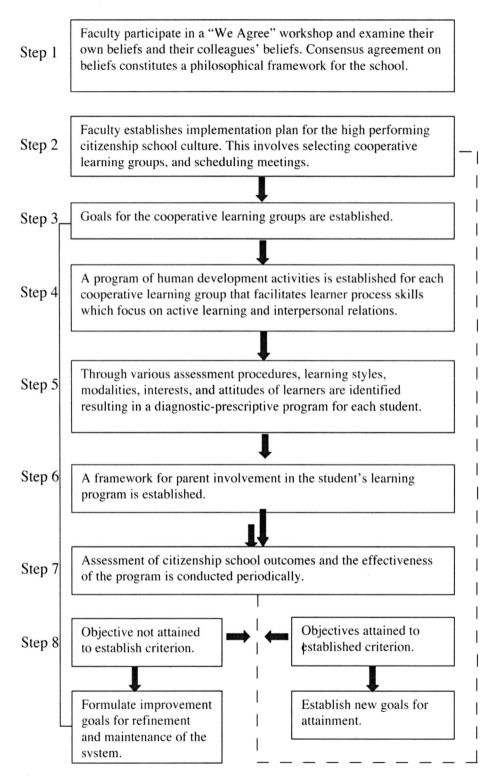

Step 1 | Faculty participate in a "We Agree" workshop and examine their own beliefs and their colleagues' beliefs. Consensus agreement on beliefs constitutes a philosophical framework for the school.

Step 2 | Faculty establishes implementation plan for the high performing citizenship school culture. This involves selecting cooperative learning groups, and scheduling meetings.

Step 3 | Goals for the cooperative learning groups are established.

Step 4 | A program of human development activities is established for each cooperative learning group that facilitates learner process skills which focus on active learning and interpersonal relations.

Step 5 | Through various assessment procedures, learning styles, modalities, interests, and attitudes of learners are identified resulting in a diagnostic-prescriptive program for each student.

Step 6 | A framework for parent involvement in the student's learning program is established.

Step 7 | Assessment of citizenship school outcomes and the effectiveness of the program is conducted periodically.

Step 8 | Objective not attained to establish criterion. | Objectives attained to established criterion.

Formulate improvement goals for refinement and maintenance of the system. | Establish new goals for attainment.

Figure 8.1

Each activity is described in a standard format. First comes the purpose, then the procedures are described in detail, and finally, there are notes to the workshop facilitator and additional suggestions, if appropriate.

DEPTH UNFOLDMENT

Activity 1: Depth Unfoldment Exercise (Castro, 1999)
Time Required: 36 minutes

Purpose

The development of a school culture in support of a high-performing school begins with the development of openness and trust among the staff. Trust is something that evolves from knowing each other and believing in each other. It is a continuous need in the relationship between faculty members since it is trust that allows successful communication, and it is through successful communication that future decisions are made. Successful communication requires both telling and listening behaviors. Activity 1 involves participants but is nonthreatening. The Depth Unfoldment Exercise's (DUE) purpose is to foster the development of trust among participants through self-disclosure.

Procedure

Form groups of five to nine participants. Give participants a fixed length of time (three minutes) to tell important facts about events in their lives. The last portion of the three minutes should be spent sharing their happiest moment in life. After the groups have finished, the group facilitator should ask the group to focus on the first person and report as much as they can remember of that person's disclosure. How well did they listen? Each member of the group should follow suit, allowing one minute for the group to focus on each person.

To the Facilitator

Some participants will find it difficult to use all of the time allocated. Others will have difficulty remaining within the time constraints. It is important to stress that each person has only three minutes to speak. Someone should alert each person when they have 30 seconds left and ask them to share their happiest moment.

Additional Suggestions

The workshop facilitator may suggest that openness to others is related to openness in themselves and that self-knowledge is a necessary requisite for full development. One final suggestion is to measure levels of openness and trust within the school, within each group, or between the principal and the faculty (Bulach, 2003). A group openness and trust survey that measures these levels is available at www.westga.edu/~cbulach. The survey measures the telling and listening dimensions of openness and the five dimensions of trust.

Activity 2: Peak Experience Method (Castro, 1999)
Time Required: 37 minutes

Purpose

Another method that is useful as a follow-up to the DUE is the Peak Experience Method. The primary purpose of the exercise, as with the DUE, is the development of self-awareness and trust among participants. This experience continues the "getting to know you process" begun in Activity 1. The Peak Experience Method helps each participant identify experiences that he or she values from this experience.

Procedure

The workshop facilitator should ask participants to share peak experiences in their lives. A peak experience is defined as an emotional high from something that gave the person a great deal of pleasure or a great feeling of accomplishment. Give participants 10 to 15 minutes to complete their response to the following peak experience for

- Last week
- Last year
- Between college and last year
- During college
- During high school
- Before high school

Then ask each participant to share their response for one of the above. After each has shared a peak experience from last week, have them share last year, etc.. This structured sharing allows each member to have a turn every few moments rather than one long turn.

To the Facilitator

Often participants will feel they have to seek very important experiences before they can share them. The workshop facilitator should share an experience with the group as an example. For example, someone might recall the time they made the honor roll and remembers the high associated with that experience. The facilitator should stress that it is not the actual event that they should concentrate on in this experience but rather the feeling that accompanies it.

Additional Suggestions

Several variations of the DUE and the Peak Experience Method can be used to develop trust and openness among group participants. These variations are discussed in Activities 3, 4, and 5 and may be used in addition to or as a substitute for the DUE and Peak Experience Method.

Activity 3: Six-by-Six Self Introduction (Castro, 1999)
Time Required: 36 minutes

Purpose

This method is similar to the DUE method. The primary purpose of the exercise is the development of trust through self-disclosure.

Procedure

Form groups of six and give each member six minutes to answer:

1. Who am I?
2. The Most Important Experiences of My Life Were . . .
3. The Happiest Moments in My Life Were . . .

Appoint a timekeeper for each group to tell members when only one minute remains so that person can share their happiest moment.

To the Facilitator

A good follow-up is going around the circle and drawing numbers or names so that each person has to remember what one of the participants in the group has said about themselves. This mirroring of what an individual has heard shows that individuals in the group were interested and listened.

Activity 4: Paired Interviews (Castro, 1999)
Time Required: 36 minutes

Purpose

The purpose of the exercise is the development of self-awareness, trust among participants, and self-disclosure.

Procedure

The workshop facilitator should introduce the exercise by asking participants to choose partners by counting off in twos or turning to the person next to them. They should interview their partners to find out as much as they can about them. They should choose someone they know the least about.

Ask the participants to take notes during the interview and ask such questions as where their partner was born, which schools they attended, how many members are in their family, what their hobbies and interests are, whether they have pets, what their achievements are, and so forth. After interviewing for 10 to 15 minutes, instruct participants to tell about the person they have interviewed. The person should stand behind their partner as they speak.

After all participants have spoken, ask the group to remember as much as they can about each person in the group. After relating the information they recall about each person, choose one person in the group. Everyone else should tell that person what they thought he or she must have been like 10 years ago.

To the Facilitator

Workshop participants may discover how well they listened or should listen and the importance of effective communication. In addition, those who are being talked about will discover that the group already knows a great deal about them.

Activity 5: Pair and Square (Castro, 1999)
Time Required: 36 minutes

Purpose

The purpose of the exercise is the development of self-awareness, trust among participants, and self-disclosure. The focus is on the telling and listening dimensions of openness which facilitate the development of trust. (Bulach, 2003)

Procedure

Ask participants to find someone in the room they do not know and attempt to get to know them. They should find out as much as possible about each other. After five minutes ask each pair to find another pair and get to know them. Allow five minutes, and ask each foursome to find another foursome and go through the same process. After 10 minutes, ask the group to discuss their differences in the various sized groups.

To the Facilitator

Pair and Square, Paired Interviews, and the Six-by-Six Self Introduction are all variations of Activities 1 and 2. Each can be used in addition to or as a substitute for the DUE and the Peak Experience Method depending on the needs of the group. The Pair and Square technique is especially useful in pointing out the differences between large and small groups.

INSTRUMENTATION

Activity 6: Fundamental Interpersonal Relations Orientation-Behavior (Schutz, 1958)
Time Required: 36 minutes

Purpose

This instrumentation and forced-choice exercise provides nonthreatening information to teachers about their own needs for working in a group setting.

Procedure

Distribute the Fundamental Interpersonal Relations Orientation-Behavior (FIRO-B) instrument. Upon completion, have workshop participants score their own instrument by providing scoring keys or by reading the scoring procedure. Next, provide newsprint and have all participants report their scores. Report your own scores as modeling behavior. Next, explain the interpretation of the scores as described below. The group should be encouraged to mingle and view other participant's scores. Allow individuals an opportunity to compare their scores with the "norm" group found in the FIRO-B manual and with each other.

Instrument

The FIRO-B was developed by William Schutz. He identifies groups and individuals as having three fundamental interpersonal needs: inclusion, control, and affection. For an individual to function optimally in a group, he or she must establish and maintain a satisfactory relation in all three areas. Individuals need to include others and be included (inclusion), to control others and be controlled (control), and to like others and be liked (affection).

The exact mix of needing or wanting in each of these dimensions varies for each person. Inclusion, control, and affection are phases through which groups must successfully pass if they are to achieve sustained effectiveness in accomplishing school goals. The first dimension that must be met is the feeling that a person is included. The second dimension is a person's need in the control dimension, and the final area is a person's need in the affection dimension.

The primary purpose of the FIRO-B instrument is to measure how a person acts in interpersonal situations and to predict their interaction with others. The FIRO-B provides a measurement of two levels of self-perceived behavior: that expressed by self and that wanted from others toward self. Each of these levels is measured along the three dimensions. The instrument consists of 54 Likert-type items measured on a six-point scale. The instrument can be purchased from Consulting Psychologist Press at 1055 Joaquin Rd Ste 200 Mountain View, 94043California USA phone (650) 969-8901. The FIRO-B website is http://www.cpp.com. There are also numerous sites on the internet where this instrument can be accessed. Just type in FIRO-B.

To the Facilitator

Results of the instrument should not be used as a diagnostic interpretation of the individual. Instead, the instrument should be used to bring the concepts of inclusion, control, and affection into self-awareness so that the dimensions are a starting point for discussion. This technique should not be attempted until the preceding activities have been completed or until a sufficient level of openness and trust has been established within the group. After members have completed the instrument, they should be given time to discuss their scores with other members. After this discussion, each group should be encouraged to share key discussion items with other groups.

Definition of the FIRO-B Factors and Scoring Interpretations

The following is a d efinition of the three variables and an explanation of extreme scores. Use good judgment in interpreting scores, and allow faculty to interpret their own scores. Please note that this is our interpretation of the scores. The interpretation provided by FIRO-B personnel may differ slightly.

- Motivation defined: Internal factors that direct or sustain a behavior. An external factor can be involved, but it serves as a stimulus for the internal factor. For example, see a vicious dog (external) fear (internal) causes a person to run. According to Schutz (1958), our behavior in groups is motivated by inclusion, control, and affection. Each has two dimensions: a) what we do (active and external) to get our needs met in this domain and b) what we want (passive and internal) to get our needs met in this domain. Consequently, each domain yields two scores: a) what a person does and b) what a person wants.
- Inclusion defined: A desire to be with other people, to be invited to join groups and organizations, and so forth. This desire is caused by our need to feel important or significant—our self-concept. It is the first interpersonal need to develop in a group. Either extreme—over social (high scores) or under social (low scores)—is caused by a feeling of worthlessness and a poor self-concept.
- Control defined: Having power, influence, or authority over others. It can range from having complete control over self and others (do) to being completely controlled (want) by others. A person can be both controlling and controlled. There is a tendency to model the behavior of the one who controls us. In a group, after inclusion issues have been worked out, the control issues are addressed.
- Affection defined: An emotional feeling that occurs between two people. Feelings can range from none to very intense, particularly in the areas of love and hate. It is the last of the three interpersonal needs to develop. Over personal (high scores) or under personal (low scores) are caused by fears of rejection.

The subscales contain nine single-statement items with scores ranging from zero to nine (Spies & Plake, 2005). Faculty members who have very low scores or very high scores for what they do to get control and what they want from others could be experiencing emotional problems. For example, faculty members who have a high need to control would have a high score on what they do. This is indicative of those who exert a lot of energy in an effort to control their environment. If these same faculty members have a high want score for their need to be in control, he or she might be experiencing a lot of anxiety and stress.

To provide a better understanding of possible scores, let's explore some extreme score patterns. These are interpretations of extreme scores—scores of nine on what a person **wants** and nine on what a person does, or scores of zero on what a person wants and zero on what a person does. These are interpretations by Bulach and others may have a slightly different interpretation of scores. The word "activity" is used for "does" scores because it shows what a person "does" in this dimension.

Inclusion Extremes

- Low scores on both dimensions, the under social or "the happy hermit": This person does not want to be included and doesn't try to include anyone.
- High scores on both dimensions, the over social or "the politician": This person always seeks the limelight and prominence. S/he puts wants to be included and puts forth a lot of effort to be included.
- High activity, low want scores, "the social butterfly": This person makes the rounds, always moving from one person to another. Loves being included, but it's his or her choice.
- Low activity, high want scores, "the wallflower": This person has a high desire to be included but will not take the initiative to get invited. This person sits and waits to be invited.

Control Extremes

- Low scores on both dimensions, "the rock": This person has no desire to be moved or controlled by anyone and has no desire to move or control anyone. They wish to be left alone. The best occupation for this person is solitary work.
- High scores on both dimensions, "the heart attack waiting to happen": This person puts forth a lot of effort to control their environment and wants very much to be in a controlled environment. They are constantly looking to experts and superiors for guidance and are fearful of making a mistake and losing control.
- High activity, low want scores, "the autocrat" or "the dictator": This person has a high need to control and refuses to be controlled by others. They tend to be a leader so they can control others. There is a tendency to be overworked because they will not delegate because no one can do it better. Subordinates are dependent and cannot grow.

- Low activity, high want scores, "the abdicrat" or "the follower": This person will not take responsibility and allows others to make all decisions. The zero-nine and the nine-zero are very compatible, but one soon loses respect for the other.

Affection Extremes

- Low scores on both dimensions, "the under personal" or "the cold fish": This person does not want or give affection.
- High scores on both dimensions, the over-personal or the "can't get enough": This person is very warm and caring and gives and receives affection but can never get enough to allay fear of rejection.
- High activity, low want scores, "the love'em and leave 'em": This person enjoys giving affection but will not allow anyone to return it for fear that they will feel obligated. This person tends to move from relationship to relationship, and as soon as their love is reciprocated, they end the relationship.
- Low activity, high want scores, "the dying on the vine": This person has difficulty being intimate. They can only receive and do not know how to give.

Other Possible Interpretations

- high inclusion scores: Indicate that people are very important
- high control scores: Indicate that a person enjoys responsibility
- high active scores: Indicate an outward active person
- high want scores: Indicate that a person is dependent on others to get what they want

Could a person who has a high need to control also have a high need to be controlled? It happens more often than one would think. There are principals with extremely controlling and autocratic styles. With this type of leader, teachers and students are never involved in the decision-making process. At the same time, this type of principal always makes sure that what she or he does meets the approval of some higher authority. Getting approval from the superintendent or board members becomes a pattern. It is not unusual for him or her to go to a conference and attend a workshop presentation by some expert on a new technique only to return to school and implement the new technique. There is a high need to control and a high need to be controlled. Their stress level is usually very high and can eventually lead to medical problems and early retirement.

Conversely, a person with low scores on the need to control and be controlled would put forth little effort to control his or her environment and would not allow others to control them. A person with a low score on his or her need to control and a high score on the need to be controlled would be easily manipulated by others. A person with a high need to control and low need to be controlled could be a team leader or a bully.

Similar patterns occur with inclusion and affection needs. A person who puts forth a lot of effort to be included in a group and has a high need for others to include them has needs that are difficult to satisfy because they will always feel that they were not included somehow. A person who exerts a lot of effort in the affection domain and has a high need for affection will also experience problems because their affection needs will never be satisfied. For example, if they are putting a lot of energy into giving affection to others, they will have difficulty getting their own affection needs met.

BRAINSTORMING

Activity 7: Brainstorming (Simon, Howe, & Kirschenbaum, 1991)
Time Required: 20 minutes

Purpose

Once the workshop facilitator has developed trust and openness among the faculty and the faculty has explored their own needs and philosophic positions using Activities 1 through 6, the group is ready for a brainstorming session. Brainstorming is one of the most effective information generating activities available. It is the process of listing all the ideas a group has concerning a specific topic.

Procedure

Before beginning the brainstorming session, the group facilitator should review the following guidelines: (a) no criticism is allowed, (b) the group should work for quantity of ideas rather than quality, and (c) the group should build on the ideas of others.

The brainstorming session should be used primarily as a tool to understand the brainstorming process and practice generating and cataloging ideas. Simulating the brainstorming technique will prove beneficial when Activity 9 is attempted. Activity 8 is the culminating activity for Component 1 of the staff development workshop.

The use of a nonsense topic, such as the uses of a safety pin, can serve as the medium for simulating the brainstorming technique. Divide the faculty into groups of six. Allow four to five minutes for the actual brainstorming experience. The groups should then be instructed to analyze their responses to the topic by noting duplications, adding, substituting, deleting, and prioritizing their statements. The statements should be recorded on a large sheet of paper with a crayon or felt-tip marker. A master list incorporating all the ideas culled from the individual small groups can then be developed and hung in front of the room for all to see.

To the Facilitator

These activities clarify the manner in which the brainstormed data are put into a usable format.

WE AGREE

Activity 8: "We Agree"
Time Required: Varies depending on the size of the faculty

Purpose

The preceding seven activities emphasize trust and openness, and self-awareness. During these exercises, the faculty both individually and as a group examined their own needs, practiced their telling and listening skills related to openness, and improved levels of trust between members. During this phase of the "We Agree" workshop, faculty members will invariably disagree on some issues. This is a positive step. Faculty members who have gone through this phase are generally open and honest with each other and view disagreement as a positive force from which future agreement can be reached. The "We Agree" Activity is a culmination of the preceding activities.

Specifically, the "We Agree" Activity will help the faculty develop statements of consensus regarding their work with students. These statements will help create environments that support and nurture the high-performing school.

Procedure

Small groups of six should be formed. If possible, no two people from the same department or area should be placed in the same group. "We Agree" statements should be developed in the small groups for the topic area, "The High-Performing School Culture." Each group should print "We Agree" and the topic of focus, for example, "The High-Performing School" on the top of a large sheet of paper with a crayon or felt-tip marker.

The faculty in each group should read chapters 1 through 5 prior to the "We Agree" meeting. During the meeting they should spend 30 to 40 minutes discussing, writing, and rewriting statements that all group members find agreeable. When all of the small groups have reached agreement on their lists, one member from each small group should meet with the facilitator to develop a master list incorporating all the ideas culled from the individual small group statements. A very important part of this discussion should be the implementation process. Do they want to do Phase I the first year and Phase II the second, Phase III the third and Phase IV the fourth year? Perhaps they want to do Phase I and Phase IV the first year, or maybe all four phases at once?

This master list should then be returned to each small group. Each group should discuss the statements on the consolidated list with the purpose of reaching a consensus. This process may require the modification and/or removal of statements. The final result is a school wide list. Through this involvement of the faculty, a philosophical framework is provided for the school, which will likely support the implementation of the high-performing school culture.

To the Facilitator

The "We Agree" Activity can be implemented over a period of days at the facilitator's discretion depending upon the availability of time. The second component of the "We Agree" workshop is concerned with the mechanics of implementing the high-performing school culture (see Step 2, Figure 8.1). Who will be involved, when will faculty support groups meet, what the teachers and administrators will do during the meetings, and who will coordinate the program are a few of the questions that should be addressed during this phase of the workshop. During this phase of the workshop, the facilitator can select exercises from chapter 9, if additional activities are needed to improve levels of openness and trust

CONCLUSION

This chapter is concerned with professional development. It presents a model for professional development and includes eight activities designed to develop openness and trust and help staff develop a philosophical framework for the school that supports the high-performing school culture. The chapter concludes with a discussion (We Agree) of the mechanics involved in implementing a high-performing school culture. The next chapter provides additional activities for the development of openness and trust. These are considered the building blocks for any effective school culture and climate.

REFERENCES

Bubb, S. (2007). *Leading and managing professional development: Developing people, developing schools*. Thousand Oaks, CA: Sage/Paul Chapman Publishing.

Bulach, C. R. (2003). The impact of human relations training on levels of openness and trust. *Research for Educational Reform* 8(4), 43–57.

Castro, S. (1999). *Self-disclosure*. San Francisco: Watermark Press.

Darling-Hammond, L. (2007). *Preparing teachers for a changing world: What teachers should learn and be able to do*. New York: John Wiley & Sons.

Lunenburg, F.C. (2001). *Development and use of the instructional programming model (IMP) to meet the individual needs of students (Tech. Rep. No. 6)*. Huntsville, TX: Sam Houston State University, Center for Research and Doctoral Studies in Educational Leadership.

National Staff Development Council. (2007). *Teachers can be leaders of change*. Washington, D.C.: National Staff Development Council.

Schutz, W. C. (1958). *FIRO: A three-dimensional theory of interpersonal behavior*. New York: Holt, Rinehart, and Winston.

Sergiovanni, T., & Starratt, R. (2006). *Supervision: A redefinition* (8th ed.). New York: McGraw-Hill.

Spies, R. A., & Plake, B. S. (2005). *The sixteenth mental measurements yearbook*. Lincoln, NE: Buros Institute of Mental Measurements.

Witmer, J. T. (2007). *Team-based professional development: A process for school reform*. Lanham, MD: Roman & Littlefield Education.

Chapter 9

Improving Levels of Openness and Trust

Effective leadership is an important requirement for the success of any new program, such as the implementation of the high-performing school. Implementation of a program involves people, and much of this involvement is in group situations. Levels of openness and trust are key components to how effectively groups function. In this chapter we will provide more activities that improve levels of openness and trust. They can be used at any time during implementation of the school reform process, that is, during year one, year two, and so on.

To illustrate the importance of these two factors, we will use the analogy of oil and water in a car engine. Oil and water in an internal combustion engine are like openness and trust in a group. Without water in the radiator of an engine, it will heat up very fast and cease to function. Without some level of openness in a group or organization, people will not talk to each other and/or will not listen to each other. People will get mad, have poor morale, and soon the group will cease to function effectively.

Without oil in an engine, it will also become very hot and cease to function. With some oil, friction is reduced, and the engine will run for quite awhile. If a degree of trust is present in a group or organization, friction or conflict is often dealt with in a constructive manner. People work together to solve the problem. Without some degree of trust, conflict quickly escalates and causes the group to become dysfunctional. Consequently, an effective leader has to create opportunities or activities that are likely to improve levels of openness and trust. This further enhances the implementation of a high performing school culture.

ACTIVITIES THAT IMPROVE OPENNESS

The following activities are designed to improve levels of openness. These same activities can be use by classroom teachers to improve levels of openness with students in the classroom setting. How students treat each other is very important for a high performing school culture. As described in chapter 8, openness has a telling and a listening dimension. A person can be very open on one dimension of openness and closed on the other. It is not uncommon for someone to be very open on the telling dimension and closed on the listening dimension. All of these activities provide opportunities to use both the telling and listening dimensions of openness.

ACTIVITY #1: POSITIVE, MINUS, INTERESTING

Required Time: 30 minutes

Purpose

The Positive, Minus, Interesting (PMI) activity provides faculty or students with the opportunity to state the positive, negative, and interesting aspects on a number of topics (telling dimension). This is a good warm up activity to use prior to a meeting. It can also be used to get feedback (listening dimension) on a variety of issues, that is, how the redirects are working, how was the open house, how discipline is being handled, and so on. This activity legitimizes stating the negative, but also forces faculty to think about the positive aspects. When asked to state the interesting, they have to focus on something that is neither positive nor negative. It is a great warm up activity and a way to get feedback!

Procedure

Form groups of four to five and instruct faculty to share positive, negative, and interesting things about the chosen topic. Instruct them to appoint a leader who will speak for the group when the activity is over.

At the classroom level, students could be asked to do a PMI on their summer vacation. They can also be asked to share information on a number of other topics, such as what they like about the class, what they think about the way the teacher teaches, their feelings about the school, their feelings about the principal, and so forth.

To the Facilitator

After 10 to 15 minutes make sure everyone has had a chance to share their PMI. Allow more time if necessary. Have each group's leader share one thing that was revealed each time their group was asked to share. When they are finished, go to one group and ask for a positive that was shared. Go to another group and ask for a minus. And go to another group and ask for an interesting thing that was shared. Continue the process with each group. When you return to the first group that shared a positive, ask them to share a minus. Vary the process so that each group has shared a PMI. A variation on this is to have each group share a positive, minus, and interesting, instead of one at a time. When all groups have contributed, ask if a group has anything else they wish to share.

ACTIVITY #2: GUESS WHO?

Required Time: 36 minutes

Purpose

This can be used as a getting-to-know-you better activity. It focuses everyone's attention on one person in a healthy way and gives that person a moment in the spotlight.

Procedure

Have the faculty get into their groups, teams, grade level or other form of organization. Each faculty member should write out some biographical information on an index card that describes them but does not make it too obvious who they are. Include such things as hobbies, talents, major trips they have taken, unusual things about their family, and so on. Collect the cards and read them while the group attempts to guess who is being described. This can be done at the school level and not the group level, depending on the size of the faculty. The same process can be used at the classroom level for students. The teacher or a student can collect the cards and read them while the class attempts to guess who is being described.

To the Facilitator of each Group

Include a card of your own.

ACTIVITY #3: GETTING TO KNOW YOU

Required Time: 36 minutes

Purpose

The Getting to Know You activity can be used at the school level for faculty and at the classroom level for students. It focuses on both the telling and listening dimensions of openness. Through participation in the activity, faculty and students learn a little more about each other. School principals might want to use it for all faculty or only for new faculty.

Procedure

Begin by welcoming everyone to the group and telling them a little about yourself. This way, they will begin to get to know you and will feel more comfortable introducing themselves once you have modeled that behavior. Next, have them arrange their chairs in a circle and write on the board or on a piece of paper:

1. Something you like to do
2. Something unique about you that others are not likely to know
3. Something you want others to know about you

Each person should be asked to repeat the sentence, "I'm _____ and I _____," completing the blanks by inserting their name and something they like to do (for example, "I'm Bill and I like to ski"), or something that is unique about them that others are not likely to know (for example, "I'm Helena and I was born in Holland"), or something they want others to know about them (for example, "I'm Tom and I'm trying to improve my communication skills").

The first person, preferably a volunteer should begin by saying his or her statement, "I'm Bill and I like to ski." The next person in the circle should then look at Bill and say, "You're Bill and you like to ski. I'm Helena and I was born in Holland." The third person in line then looks first at Bill, then at Helena, saying, "You're Bill and you like to ski. You're Helena and you were born in Holland. I'm Tom and I'm trying to improve my communication skills." This procedure should continue around the entire circle.

To the Facilitator

This activity helps people remember each other's names. It also provides some meaningful associations, which can be used to begin conversations and get to know one another outside the group. "Hey, Bill, I like to ski, also." "Helena, how long did you live in Holland?" "Don't worry, Tom, I want to improve my communication skills, too."

ACTIVITY #4: NAME TAGGING (JOHNSON, 2005)

Required Time: 36 minutes

Purpose

The purpose of the Name Tagging exercise is to get to know other members of the group, no matter how large, relax a bit, and begin to get acquainted. This activity is a variation of the previous exercise.

Procedure

Instruct everyone to write their first name in the center of a 3 × 5 index card. They should write large so it can be read at some distance. In the upper left hand corner, they should write the names of their birthplace and their favorite place. In the upper right hand corner, they should write two of their favorite activities, whether they are sports, hobbies, pastimes, jobs, or other leisure activities. In the lower left hand corner, they should write three adjectives that describe them. And in the lower right-hand corner, they should describe something they are looking forward to and something they are excited about doing in the future, for example, a vacation. They should then pin the card on the front of their shirts and mill around, finding people they don't know and discussing each other's cards. They should try to meet as many people as possible in the time allowed (about 20 minutes).

To the Facilitator

Request that everyone keep their name tags and wear them at subsequent sessions until everyone knows each other. A sample index card appears in Figure 9.1.

```
Louisiana                    Skiing

Switzerland                  Writing

                Fred

Task-oriented                Skiing

Intense                          in

Hard-working                 Chile
```

Figure 9.1

ACTIVITY #5: ONE SPECIAL THING

Required Time: 36 minutes

Purpose

This activity builds rapport and improves morale between members of the group. It creates opportunities to practice both the listening and telling dimensions of openness. This can also be used as a classroom activity.

Procedure

Divide the group into pairs. Instruct them to carry on a normal conversation for five minutes, each person telling the other as much as possible about himself or herself. Ask them to choose things about themselves that they think are important to share. After five minutes, bring the group back together as one large group (preferably in a circle). Then ask each person to introduce his or her partner by stating their partner's name and the one special thing that impressed them most about that person.

To the Facilitator

The discussion can be ended (optional) by asking the group to talk about what it was like to talk to the other person and what it was like to be talked about in the group.

ACTIVITY #6: DEPTH UNFOLDMENT EXERCISE

Required Time: 36 minutes

Purpose

The purpose of this activity is to acquaint the group with the concept of self-disclosure. Self-disclosure is an openness activity that leads to the development of trust.

Procedure

The Depth Unfoldment Exercise (DUE) was discussed in chapter 8 (activity 1). Refer to this activity for a full description of the procedure. The procedure can be adapted to the age level of any group.

To the Teacher

Refer to chapter 8 for additional tips and suggestions on how to use this strategy.

ACTIVITIES THAT IMPROVE TRUST

All of the previous activities for openness also foster the development of trust, according to the research of Bulach (1974) since openness and trust are positively related (P <.001). These activities are designed to build an open, honest, and trusting climate. This level of trust is established when the members of a group are willing to work cooperatively to improve themselves and others within the group.

If these activities are used at the classroom level, the teacher should alert students that improper touching will not be tolerated. The teacher should also be aware that physical strength can be a factor with some of the strategies. Some strategies may be more appropriate for athletic teams than for classroom groups. Proper judgment is advised.

ACTIVITY #7: TRUST FALL (JOHNSON, 2005)

Required Time: 36 minutes

Purpose

The sense of physical support can be as powerful a developer of trust as a sense of emotional support. Trust Fall is a nonverbal exercise related to the development of trust.

Procedure

Have groups form a circle facing inward with one group member in the center of the circle with his or her eyes closed. Instruct participants to fall in any direction keeping their bodies stiff and erect with their feet in the center of the circle. The group should support them and keep them moving, pushing them across to other members. Another approach is to have one member stand on a platform or stump approximately three feet off the ground. Form two lines facing inward behind them with everyone's arms stretched out and palms up. The "falling" participants should cross their arms over their chest, close their eyes, stiffen their body, and lean backward.

To the Facilitator

After completing the exercise, ask the group: How did it feel to fall? Did you doubt that the group would catch you? How did it feel to catch the participants? Did you doubt that you would be able to catch them? How has trust in the individuals who caught you been affected?

ACTIVITY #8: BLIND WALK (JOHNSON, 2005)

Required Time: 36 minutes

Purpose

Blind Walk is another nonverbal exercise related to the development of trust.

Procedure

Have each member of the group pair off with another person. One person is designated the guide and the other is the blind person. The guide should grasp the wrists of the blind person (who closes his eyes) and guide the blind person around the room touching various objects in process. After ten minutes, reverse roles and repeat.

To the Teacher

After everyone has been both a guide and a blind person, discuss the following questions in the group as a whole: How did it feel to be the blind person? How did it feel to be the guide? What did you learn about the guide? What did you learn about the blind person? How do the two of you feel about each other?

ACTIVITY #9: EXPERIMENT IN COOPERATION: THE SQUARES GAME (GAJEWSKI, 1998)

Required Time: 36 minutes

Purpose

The purpose of this activity is twofold: to analyze certain aspects of cooperation in solving a group problem and to become more sensitive to the way one's behavior may help or hinder joint problem solving.

Procedure

Before the activity, prepare a set of squares and an instruction sheet for each group. Divide the class into groups of five, and seat each group at a table supplied with a set of envelopes and an instruction sheet. Ask that the envelopes be opened only on signal. Begin the exercise by asking what cooperation means. List the requirements for cooperation on the board. For example:

1. Everyone has to understand the problem.
2. Everyone needs to believe that he or she can help.
3. Instructions need to be clear.
4. Everyone needs to think of the other person as well as themselves. Describe the experiment as a puzzle that can be solved only by cooperation. Read the instructions and rules aloud and then give the signal to open the envelopes.

Preparation of Puzzle

A puzzle set consists of five envelopes containing pieces of stiff paper cut into patterns that will create five six-inch squares. Cut the squares into parts and lightly pencil the letters "a" through "j," as shown in Figure 9.2. Then mark the envelopes A through E and distribute the pieces as described in Figure 9.2. For example, envelope A should have the pieces j, h, & e.

Erase the small letters on the pieces and instead write the envelope letters A through E so that the pieces can be easily returned for reuse. Several combinations of the pieces will form one or two squares, but only one combination will form five squares.

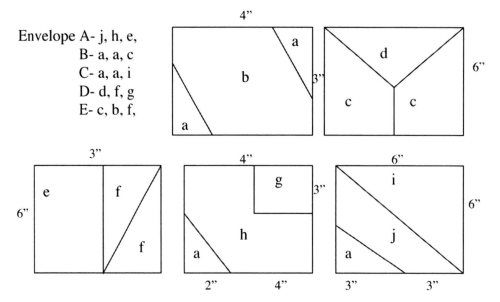

Envelope A- j, h, e,
B- a, a, c
C- a, a, i
D- d, f, g
E- c, b, f,

Figure 9.2

Directions

Each person should have an envelope containing three pieces that do not form a square. At the signal, the task of the group is to form five squares of equal size. The task is not complete until everyone has a perfect square and all the squares are of the same size.

Rules:

1. No member may speak.
2. No member may signal in any way that he or she wants a card.
3. Members may give cards or pieces to others, but no one may take a piece of a card from another.
4. They may point to their own card, but not to someone else's.

To the Facilitator

When all or most of the groups have finished, call time and discuss the experience. Ask: Who was willing to give away pieces of the puzzle? Did anyone try to violate the rules by talking or pointing as a means of helping fellow members solve their puzzles?

ACTIVITY # 10: NONVERBAL TRUST (GAJEWSKI, 1998)

Required Time: 36 minutes

Purpose

The purpose of this exercise is to become more cognizant of nonverbal ways people communicate emotions. Being able to communicate emotions nonverbally is much better than expressing them verbally. For example, if a person is frustrated there is a tendency to express it verbally with a judgment such as "That was a stupid thing to do!"

Procedure

Form a circle and deal out a deck of ordinary playing cards until everyone in the circle has the same number of cards and there are at least three cards left in the deck. Place the deck of remaining cards facedown in the center of the circle. The first person to get rid of all his or her cards is the winner. They get rid of their cards by correctly identifying the emotions expressed by other players and by accurately communicating emotions to the other players.

They should take turns expressing one emotion. To begin, the player on the dealer's left should select a card from their own hand and lay it facedown in front of them. The player should select an emotion they believe they can express based on the chart of emotions represented by each card. This chart should be posted for all to see! See below for the emotions represented by each card.

This person is now the expresser, and the remaining players should guess the emotion she or he expresses. That person should express the feeling represented by the card placed facedown. The other players should check their hands to see if they have a card that matches the expressed emotion. If they have that card, they should place the card (or cards) facedown in front of them. If they do not have the card, they should pass.

When all the cards are down for the first round, they should all be turned face up at once. If one or more of the receivers have matched the expresser's card, the expresser should put his card and all the matching cards facedown on the bottom of the deck. Any of the players who put down a wrong card must return it to their hand and draw an additional card from the top of the deck. They should draw the same number of cards from the deck that they put down in front of them.

If no other player matches the expresser's card, then the expresser has failed to communicate, and he or she should return the card to their hand and draw a penalty card from the deck. In this case, the receivers return their cards to their hands but do not draw penalty cards. If they are holding two or three cards of the same emotion, they must play all the cards if they play one of them. As expresser or receiver, they can get rid of two or three cards, or they may have to draw two or three penalty cards.

The expresser may use any nonverbal behavior he or she wishes to communicate the emotion they are portraying. No vocal clues may be used. No words may be spoken. They can use their hands, head, or whole body, and they can involve other players by touching them or engaging them in a nonverbal interchange.

Make a chart and post it of the emotions the cards represent as follows:

2 contentment
3 shyness
4 indifference
5 fear
6 frustration
7 loneliness
8 sorrow
9 anger
10 hope
Jack happiness
Queen joy
King warmth
Ace love

To the Facilitator

Explain that it is important that the expresser choose a card for an emotion that they believe they can express non-verbally. Fear, for example, is easy to express. A decision on whether to practice how to express these emotions is up to the facilitator. If the participants are unable to non-verbally express certain emotions, some practice may be necessary.

CONCLUSION

In this chapter, 10 openness and trust activities are presented. The activities are designed to provide opportunities to get to know each other on a more personal level. The major goal is to create groups that function more effectively together. Creating a high performing school with high performing classrooms requires a certain degree of openness and trust. These activities also create a role for the facilitator to come across as a servant leader, which is a key component of creating a high performing school culture. In chapter 10, we conclude our efforts to create a high performing school by creating a setting where we trust students to take charge of their own education.

REFERENCES

Bulach, C. R. (1974). *An investigation of group openness and group trust to group decisions involving risk*, (Unpublished doctoral dissertation, University of Cincinnati, 1974).

Gajewski, N. (1998). *Social skill strategies: A social-emotional curriculum for adolescents.* Greenville, SC: Super Duper Publications.

Johnson, D. W. (2005). *Reaching out: Interpersonal effectiveness and self-actualization.* Boston: Allyn & Bacon.

Chapter 10

Conferencing: Reporting Student Progress

One of the major functions of the high performing school is to provide opportunities for students to become self-directed learners. The task of the teacher is to move the learner from a stage of dependence to independence so that the learner will gradually but eventually reach the point where s/he no longer needs the teacher and can set and pursue his/her own learning goals and solve problems. A technique that facilitates this task is one that allows students to assume greater responsibility for monitoring and reporting their own progress in school.

For many years, teachers have conducted parent teacher conferences in schools for the purpose of reporting pupil progress to parents. Since the student's progress is the topic of discussion during these conferences, who knows more about it than the student? Should they not be part of the conference? This is particularly true if the teacher and student are planning, agreeing upon, and assessing the student's learning progress. These conferences need to be age appropriate. It may not be appropriate for a first grade student to be part of a conference, but we think it would be appropriate for a third or fourth grader. Teachers should use good judgment on age appropriateness. We have expressed the importance of trust in creating a high performing school culture. We think it is time to trust our students to play a major role in their parent teacher conference.

A three way parent teacher conference is an important component of the high performing school culture. Here the pupil takes an active role in reporting his/her own progress to parents. The teacher's task is to guide and direct this activity.

THREE-WAY CONFERENCES

Advocates of student led parent-teacher conferences (Bailey, 2000; Kinney, 2000; Pierce-Picciotto, 1997), whose Effectiveness Training have helped countless parents and teachers improve their communication with young people, point out that teachers who have tried three-way conferences report positive results. The benefits that have been reported are the following:

- Greater feelings of security on the part of students.
- Better use of time, less wandering from the topic.
- More complete information for the parent.
- Opportunity to facilitate the resolution of parent-student disagreements.
- Less chance of misunderstanding, everyone hears the views of the others directly.
- Better planning for future learning.
- Greater feelings of parent-child unity.
- Educative process is more likely to be regarded as cooperative rather than competitive.
- Increased desire by the student to carry out decisions, since he participated in making them.
- Increased feelings of cooperation by all participants.

The procedure for scheduling and conducting these conferences should be set by each individual school in order to meet local needs. One model for conducting parent and student-teacher conferences has been proposed by Lunenburg (2000). The model includes three components:

- Preparing for conferences,
- the conference itself, and
- the post-conference meeting.

The present description will be directed toward the role of the teacher in preparing students for the conference, the role of the teacher and student during the conference, and the post-conference meeting between the teacher and his students.

PREPARING FOR CONFERENCES

Several weeks prior to the start of the parent and student-teacher conferences, teachers may want to devote their group meetings to preparing their students for the conferences. During the semester, the teacher and his/her students have discussed many issues in the cooperative learning group meetings and in individual conferences with students. Topics such as course selection, grades, interests, attitudes, abilities, values, and meeting specific objectives should have been discussed in these sessions.

As part of the planning process for the parent and student-teacher conference, the teacher and student should discuss the content of the upcoming conference. The student is a critical part of the planning process, which involves selecting items to be mentioned at the conference and deciding how each item is to be presented. Basically, the pre-conference training meetings between the teacher and student concern two broad areas: Academic performance and social behavior.

The role of the teacher during the pre-conference meeting(s) is to help the student identify topics to be discussed and plan strategies to be used in presenting the topics at the conference. Specifically, the teacher and student should review his/her progress and set goals for the conference. The discussion should focus on attainment of objectives since the last report period, work samples to be shared with parents, test results, rate of progress, and educational goals set for the next reporting period.

Nothing should be mentioned at the parent and student-teacher conference that has not been discussed and agreed to by the teacher and student at the pre-conference meeting. This notion may be difficult to accept for some teachers. However, consider the importance of the relationship between the teacher and student. Considerable attention has been devoted to establish trust and rapport between teacher and student. Remember that the teacher is a servant leader, whose primary objective is to meet the needs of the student.

The teacher must continue to be the servant leader and build an open, honest, trusting relationship with his/her students as they plan together for the three-way conference. The student should never be surprised at a parent and student-teacher conference. This does not imply that negative aspects of the progress report should be avoided. On the contrary, negative aspects of a student's performance must be addressed. Parents have a right to know everything relative to their child's progress in school, positive as well as negative. However, every effort should be made to have the student state all negatives to the parent(s). If a student will not do that, they should be informed that the teacher will.

Pre-Conference Planning Activities

Several activities or approaches to student-pre-conference planning are presented on the following pages. The goal of the Pre-Conference Preparation Worksheet (Figure 10.1) is for the student to prepare some topics to discuss with his/her parents during a conference. The time required to complete the worksheet varies from 15–45 minutes, depending on the needs of the student. The task is best handled in an individual conference rather than a group meeting.

Figure 10.1

Pre-Conference Preparation Worksheet

Name:_____ Teacher:_____

A. List 10 facts or skills you did not know or could not do before this semester.

    1. _____

    2. _____

    3. _____

    4. _____

    5. _____

    6. _____

    7. _____

    8. _____

    9. _____

    10. _____

B. Write a short paragraph describing something you did or something that happened to you that you feel good about and are proud of.

C. List three or four things you did which have enabled you to gain in maturity and give a specific example.

D. What one thing was the single most positive thing that happened during this semester?

E. What regrets do you have about the events of the past two weeks? (This is where the negatives can be shared)

The Parent Information Worksheet (Figure 10.2) can help the student determine what topics may be in a parent and student-teacher conference. An individual conference or small group meeting is recommended for the completion of this activity. Allow approximately 10–30 minutes to complete the task.

For many students and parents, the idea of school conferences is threatening and often filled with negative overtones. It need not be. There is much a teacher can do to eliminate this fear. First, s/he can arrange conferences more frequently, making certain that some are solely for positive feedback to the parent. Secondly, s/he can give increasing control of the conference to the student, helping him/her to prepare with activities such as this one: At least one week prior to the conference, help your student complete the Student Worksheet for Parent Conference (Figure 10.3). This activity will help a student generate and organize positive information in preparation for a parent conference. An individual or small group meeting will best facilitate the completion of this task.

Figure 10.2

The Parent Information Worksheet

1. List at least five items that you think your parents would be interested in discussing in a three-way conference with you and your teacher.

   a.

   b.

   c.

   d.

   e.

2. What other items might you wish to discuss at the conference?

3. Do you and your parents have general agreement about your school program and objectives?

4. Do you and your parents have special problems or concerns about any aspects of your schooling? Please specify.

Figure 10.3

Student Worksheet for Parent Conference

I. Past and Present Achievements

    A. What is the **best** thing that's happened to you at school during the last month?

    B. List your classes. Mention some skill or idea that you have acquired and that you have enjoyed for each class.

       1.

       2.

       3.

       4.

       5.

       6.

       7.

    C. List **examples** of your work that you would like to bring to your conference.

    D. List other **activities** that are part of your daily routine. What do you like about these?

II. Present Attitudes

    A. I've improved the most in _____
because

    B. I was surprised about myself in _____
because

    C. I know the information I have from _____
will be useful to me later because_____

    D. To me grades are _____ because _____

(Continued)

Figure 10.3 (Continued)

III. Future Plans

    A. What do you want to accomplish during the next semester?

    B. What is one thing you'll do to achieve your goal(s)?

    C. What can the school do to help you meet your goal(s)?

    D. What can your parents do to help you meet your goal(s)?

    E. Other:

The teacher will want to give his/her students the opportunity to provide feedback, which can be used in a three-way conference. The Teacher Comment Form (Figure 10.4) can facilitate this process. The teacher simply sends the form to other teachers to comment on the student's learning program, his/her progress, needs, and interests. The statements entered on the form will assist in preparing for the parent and student-teacher conference.

Figure 10.4

Teacher Comment Form

Directions: Would you please take a moment to respond to the points checked below. This will help me in planning for the upcoming parent and student-teacher conference. It will be helpful if a greater emphasis is placed on the **positive**. Please make your descriptions as brief and concise as possible and place in my mailbox as soon as completed. Thank you!

Student Name: _____ Date:_____

Teacher Name: _____ Course:_____

_____ 1. Is s/he attending class regularly?

_____ 2. Have you assigned any homework? Circle one: Yes No Does s/he complete his/her homework? _____

_____ 3. Does s/he work well independently or in groups?

_____ 4. Does s/he need close supervision?

(Continued)

Figure 10.4 (Continued)

_____   5. Does s/he have a learning handicap or deficiency that you are aware of? If so, what do you suggest for help in this area?

_____   6. Does s/he have difficulty reading materials in your subject? If so, have you contacted the reading teacher for help or materials?

_____   7. What do you think are his/her chances of succeeding in additional or more advanced courses in your subject area?

_____   8. How does s/he participate in class?

_____   9. What seems to be his/her most outstanding academic ability?

_____   10. What seems to be his/her most outstanding personal quality?

_____   11. What has s/he done in class that s/he should be particularly proud of?

_____   12. Other: _____

During a large or small group meeting, the teacher may wish to simulate a parent and student-teacher conference. The teacher might have the student role play his/her parent, or the teacher might have a few students role play in front of the group. Another variation is to have the cooperative learning group be the parent to ask questions of one or more students. The goal is to provide an opportunity for the student to learn to conduct his/her own conferences. About 45 minutes are required to complete the activity.

Practicing the Conference

Procedure

1. Divide the class into groups of three. Each would play a role representing the parent, the teacher, and the student. (Teacher might play himself as well.)
2. Rotate the role so each student has an opportunity to be the student or him or herself in the conference.
3. Student should start the conference as it would be in the actual situation following the prescribed organization.
4. Here is a list of possible questions that a parent of a high school student might ask:
   a. How's _____ doing this year in school?

b. What are the graduation requirements?

c. Will any courses count _____ at the university?

d. But, how come we had to come in and sit here just to hear how well he's doing? What are the problems? My parents never heard from the school unless there was something wrong.

e. How's _____ attendance been? Is s/he cutting any classes?

f. What are the differences among the programs that place students outside the school for part of their time?

g. How may my child get credit if s/he isn't in school?

h. Why aren't you taking a full year of American History now?

i. Don't you have to take Junior English?

j. How will my child learn the educational "basics?"

k. What if _____ fails a course?

The teacher can devise his/her own questions to accommodate the needs and purposes of their grade level and school. The activities and approaches to pre-conference planning were not meant to be exhaustive. Others can be devised by teachers to meet individual teacher needs. As a final pre-conference planning activity, the teacher is encouraged to use a guide to assess the student's readiness for reporting progress at a parent and student-teacher conference. Figure 10.5 is an example of such a guide.

Figure 10.5

Guidelines for Assessing Student Readiness to Report His/Her Progress

Student's name: _____ Date: _____

Check One:	Satisfactory	Needs Improvement
1. Reports his/her general progress to teacher.	_____	_____
2. Gives specific examples of attainment of objectives in all areas.	_____	_____
3. Selects representative work samples to share and discuss with parent.	_____	_____
4. Shares and interprets test results.	_____	_____

(Continued)

Figure 10.5 (Continued)

5. Reports rate of progress to teacher.   _____   _____

6. Interprets progress on group charts.   _____   _____

7. Indicates reasons for not attaining some goals.   _____   _____

8. Sets educational goals to be attained.   _____   _____

9. Discusses how new educational goals will be attained.   _____   _____

10. When teacher poses question concerning progress, the student responds with appropriate information.   _____   _____

11. Other_____

THE CONFERENCE MEETING

Each school will need to develop its own plan for parent and student-teacher conferences suited to local needs. Every school community is somewhat different and may have needs not found elsewhere. Some things to bear in mind when planning conferences are listed below.

1. Make certain conferences are scheduled so as to allow both parents to be present. It is a good idea to provide parents with the option of a day or evening conference.
2. A major component of a high performing school is the three- way conference; therefore, it is essential that students be free of other obligations so that they can be present at the conference. Make sure another important school district event is not planned for the date of the conference. For example, a parent may have a student in another school who is in a school play or football game.
3. Schedule conferences so that parents are provided at least 30 minutes to discuss their child's progress; in addition, structure each conference so that parents have some time to ask questions and/or provide comments.

4. Make certain notices of the conferences are provided to all parties at least one week in advance of the meeting date, and provide some mechanism whereby parents can indicate whether or not they will attend.
5. Provide for the evaluation of individual and overall conferences through means of anonymous questionnaires; to assure anonymity a receptacle can be placed at the conference site in which the completed questionnaires can be deposited by the respondents.

Evaluation forms which were used by one of the authors (Lunenburg) used (Figures 10.6 and 10.7) while he served as a high school principal and later as superintendent of schools of a suburban public school district are provided below. Figure 10.6 is completed by the teacher, and Figure 10.7 is completed by the parent.

Figure 10.6

Evaluation of Parent/Student/Teacher Conferences Report Form

Teacher _____ Date _____

Conference Dates _____ Unit/Grade/Department _____

Information Item	**Response**	
Elementary:		
Unit/Grade Enrollment	_____	
Secondary:		
Teacher's Total Student Enrollment	_____	
Type of conferences held: (Circle response)		
Parent/teacher?	Yes	No
Parent/teacher/student?	Yes	No
Both options open to parents?	Yes	No
Total number of conferences held:		
Number with mother only present	_____	
Number with father only present	_____	
Number with both parents present	_____	
Number with student and mother present	_____	

(Continued)

Figure 10.6 (Continued)

Number with student and father present	_____
Number with student and both parents present	_____
Number of conferences held: Total	_____
Before 4:30 p.m.	_____
Between 4:30 p.m. and 7:00 p.m.	_____
After 7:00 p.m.	_____
Before 8:00 a.m.	_____

Figure 10.7

PARENT REACTION TO THE PARENT AND STUDENT-TEACHER CONFERENCES

Circle which grades: I have students in Grades K 1 2 3 4 5 6 7 8 9 10 11 12
Directions: We would appreciate your giving us your reaction to the Parent and Student- Teacher Conference procedures. Your name is not needed. Check a point on the scale below as to your perception of the degree the conference was helpful.

	Very Helpful	Helpful	Little Help	No Help
	4	3	2	1
1. Conference scheduling procedures	4	3	2	1
2. Understanding of the goals and purposes of the conferences	4	3	2	1
3. Knowing the academic skills of' your child	4	3	2	1
4. Knowing the social skills of your child	4	3	2	1
5. Knowing the attitudes reflected in school by your child	4	3	2	1

(Continued)

Figure 10.7 (Continued)

6. Knowing the compara-
   tive achievement of
   your child   4   3   2   1

Express any additional concerns or unanswered questions in the space below. Please state your thoughts on whether the conferences should be continued or not. _____

_____

Evaluation forms such as these can provide valuable information to a school administrator concerning the number of conferences held, most popular time periods, and teacher and parent reaction to conferences. Such feedback can also be used to evaluate the success of one component of the high performing school program—the three-way conference. These forms can be modified anyway you wish. If you do not want to use these forms, consider using the force field analysis process described in chapter 2.

After students have spent a week or two preparing for the conference, the teacher should discuss ground rules for behavior during the conference. The following rules can be discussed during advisory meetings preceding the conference (Lunenburg, 2000):

1. The purpose of the conference is to support the student's progress and show specific examples of such progress.
2. Attacking and criticizing individual teachers or other students is not part of the process and is not to be allowed.
3. Student participation is critical and many points to be discussed are to be led by the advisee.
4. The parent is to be respected at all times and being courteous and thoughtful is expected.
5. The teacher must use self-discipline to keep control of the conference. Becoming defensive is not beneficial to problem-solving.
6. Listen to what the parents have to say on the points being discussed and encourage the parents to take an active part in the total conference process.
7. Keep a written agenda for the conference in order to make sure that the key points are mentioned. The teacher should make sure the conference stays on task and accomplishes the issues agreed upon at the pre-conference meeting between the advisor and student.
8. Be clear on academic performance progress, so the parent knows exactly where the student is performing.

9. Write out any questions the parent raises that cannot be answered immediately and state when and how the student or teacher is to relate the needed information.
10. Allow time at the end of the conference for parents to bring up anything that they might want to that has not been discussed earlier.
11. Make generous use of paraphrasing for miscommunications.

Conference Format

Many variations are possible for conducting a parent and student-teacher conference. The following format is recommended:

1. The student introduces the teacher to his parents.
2. The student explains the purpose of the conference to the parents.
3. The student shares and discusses representative work samples as examples of academic progress.
4. The student reports rate of progress to parents; s/he may use group charts to interpret progress or arrange work samples chronologically to make progress clear.
5. The learner shares and interprets test results as examples of level of attainment of learning objectives.
6. The student indicates reasons for not attaining some goals.
7. The student explains the rationale underlying the courses and learning activities involved in the course work and shares educational goals and discusses how these goals will be attained.
8. When parents pose questions concerning progress, the student responds with appropriate information.

It is important for the teacher to begin the conference with a positive comment about the student. This will set the tone for the overall meeting. It will allow for more effective communication on difficult issues discussed later. As the student reports his/her successes, parents who might have been negative may begin to manifest feelings of pride over their child's accomplishments.

POST-CONFERENCE MEETING

After the parent and student-teacher conference, the teacher and student should meet. At this meeting, the teacher ascertains the student's perception and overall feeling of the conference. An individual conference is recommended. However, if time constraints do not permit an individual conference, we suggest using the Positive, Minus, Interesting (PMI) activity described in chapter 9. This is a group activity and should only require 15–30 minutes to process the post-conference meeting.

Frequently the three-way conference enables families to learn more about their children than would occur at a two-way conference. Follow-up parent conversations with their children at home often result after the conference, because parents become more aware of what is occurring at school, which constitutes a major portion of a child's day.

When the student plays an active role in the conference, s/he is better able to understand the reasons why certain topics are discussed in cooperative learning group meetings and the reason why academic and social behavior goals are identified and assessed. The three-way conference has a way of integrating and synthesizing learning acquired during cooperative learning group meetings and in other classroom experiences.

Few school activities can replace the experience of personally explaining one's performance or lack of it to one's parents. The personal growth and development a student gains from being involved in a reporting process that requires self-analysis and self-evaluation (reflection) is invaluable. The goal of education is to help students become good citizens who are self-reliant learners. They are supposed to pursue their own learning and be able to monitor, report, and evaluate their own progress. The three-way conference is one way of showing students that we trust them to be able to do this.

SUMMARY

It was noted that one of the major functions of the high performing school program is to teach students to become independent learners and good citizens. A related outcome suggested was that learners assume greater responsibility for monitoring and reporting their own progress in school. A unique feature of the high performing school program is the parent and student-teacher (three-way conference). Here the pupil takes an active role in reporting his/her progress to parents, with the guidance and support of the teacher.

A model for conducting three-way conferences was presented. The model proposed included three elements: preparing for conferences, the conference itself, and the post-conference meeting. The role of the teacher and student during each of the three phases of the three-way conference was discussed. Due to time constraints, teachers should decide which of the steps need to be taken and which students are capable of conducting the three-way conference. It might be advisable to start with 6–10 students, and then add more as you become comfortable with the process.

The overall goal of the high performing school program is the improvement of the school's learning environment or culture and the graduation of students who are good citizens. Berger (2003) had this to say about implementing such a culture: "Many people want to know where to begin. Of course there is no answer to this. Every school is different. There are many entry points. A school or a classroom needs to choose a focus to begin. Start small, I suggest. It is better to improve one aspect of a culture and do it really well than to take on too much too soon and do it poorly." (p.152)

We suggest starting with Phase I and perhaps Phase IV. Parts of Phase II could also be implemented. One implementation procedure might be to present the high performing school concept to your faculty and let them decide the entry point. We do have a power point that you may use for the presentation. Send an e-mail to bulach@comcast.net and he will attach it to you. Implementation of all four or selected phases of part I of this book, followed by some of the strategies and processes presented in parts II and III, will create the culture for a high performing school. If school officials are looking for a complete school reform process: This is it!

REFERENCES

Bailey, J. (2000). *Implementing student-led conferences.* Thousand Oaks, CA: Corwin Press.

Berger, R. (2003). *An ethic of excellence: Building a culture of craftsmanship with students.* Portsmouth, NH: Heineman.

Kinney, P. (2000). *A school-wide approach to student-led conferences: A practitioner's guide.* Westerville, OH: National Middle School Association.

Lunenburg, F.C. (2000). *Designing successful parent-student-teacher conferences: Planning, implementation, and follow-up* (Tech. Rep. No. 2). Huntsville, TX: Sam Houston State University, Center for Research and Doctoral Studies in Educational Leadership.

Pierce-Picciotto, L. (1997). *Student-led parent conferences.* Jefferson City, MO: Scholastic, Inc.

About the Authors

Clete Bulach is associate professor emeritus at the University of West Georgia and the CEO of the Professional Development and Assessment Center. The agency provides training to improve leadership skills in human relations, conflict management, and group management. He has developed surveys to collect data on school climate and culture, leadership behavior, teacher caring behaviors, bullying behavior, character-related behavior, and levels of openness and trust. Manuscripts that describe research conducted with these data collection surveys can be found on his website at www.westga.edu/~cbulach. He has many publications including 37 citations in the ERIC data base. Prior to forming the consulting agency and retiring from the professoriate in 2003, he served as a superintendent (14 years), school administrator, and teacher in Ohio and retired after 30 years service in 1990. His e-mail address is cbulach@comcast.net.

Fred C. Lunenburg is the Jimmy N. Merchant Professor of Education and Senior Fellow in the Center for Research and Doctoral Studies in Educational Leadership at Sam Houston State University. Prior to moving to the university, he served as a teacher, principal, and superintendent of schools in New Jersey, Minnesota, and Wisconsin. He has authored or co-authored more than 100 articles and 20 books, including *Education Administration: Concepts and Practices* (Thomson/Wadsworth, 1991, 1996, 2000, 2004, 2008), *The Principalship: Vision to Action* (Thomson/Wadsworth, 2006), *Shaping the Future* (Rowman & Littlefield, 2003), *The Changing World of School Administration* (Rowman & Littlefield, 2002), and *High Expectations: An Action Plan for Implementing Goals 2000* (Corwin Press, 2000). He received the Phi Delta Kappa Research Award in 1986 and was the Distinguished Visiting

Professor at the University of Utrecht (The Netherlands) in 1995. His e-mail address is edu_fcl@SHSU.EDU.

Les Potter is an associate professor and the academic chair of the College of Education at Daytona State College, Daytona Beach, Florida 32114. Les has been principal of four high schools and three middle schools in four states. He was selected Principal of the Year for the State of South Carolina and North Carolina. He has as had various roles in education during his 41+ years in public education. Additionally, Les has been a tenure track professor in Educational Leadership and Foundations at the University of South Alabama and the University of West Georgia. Les has over 80 books, chapters, book reviews, and articles published in numerous educational journals. He is a reviewer and editor for *Eye on Education* and *Education Digest*. His e-mail address is potterl@DaytonaState.edu.

CPSIA information can be obtained at www.ICGtesting.com
Printed in the USA
BVOW020757270911

272155BV00001B/2/P